50 Walks in
BRECON BEACONS
& SOUTH WALES

50 Walks of 2–10 Miles

Contents

The Walks

Following the Walks

An information panel for each walk shows its relative difficulty, the distance and total amount of ascent. An indication of the gradients you will encounter is shown by the rating ▲▲▲ (no steep slopes) to ▲▲▲ (several very steep slopes). Each walk is rated for its relative difficulty compared to the other walks in this book. Walks marked +++ and colour-coded green are likely to be shorter and easier with little total ascent. Those marked with +++ and colour-coded orange are of intermediate difficulty. The hardest walks are marked +++ and colour-coded red.

MAPS

There are 40 maps, covering the 50 walks. Some walks have a suggested option in the same area. The information panel for these walks will tell you how much extra walking is involved. On short-cut suggestions the panel will tell you the total distance if you set out from the start of the main walk. Where an option returns to the same point on the main walk, just the distance of the loop is given. Where an option leaves the main walk at one point and returns to it at another, then the distance shown is for the whole walk. The minimum time suggested is for reasonably fit walkers and doesn't allow for stops. Each walk has a suggested map.

ROUTE MAP LEGEND

_ _ ▶ _ _	Walk Route	☐	Built-up Area
❶	Route Waypoint	☐	Woodland Area
– – –	Adjoining Path	🛉🛉	Toilet
＼￯／	Viewpoint	P	Car Park
●	Place of Interest	🖻	Picnic Area
⌂	Steep Section	)(	Bridge

START POINTS

The start of each walk is given as a six-figure grid reference prefixed by two letters indicating which 100km square of the National Grid it refers to. You'll find more information on grid references on most Ordnance Survey, AA Walking and Leisure Maps.

DOGS

We have tried to give dog owners useful advice about how dog friendly each walk is. Please respect other countryside users. Keep your dog under control, especially around livestock, and obey local bylaws and other dog control notices.

CAR PARKING

Many of the car parks suggested are public, but occasionally you may find you have to park on the roadside or in a lay-by. Please be considerate when you leave your car, ensuring that access roads or gates are not blocked and that other vehicles can pass safely.

WALKS LOCATOR

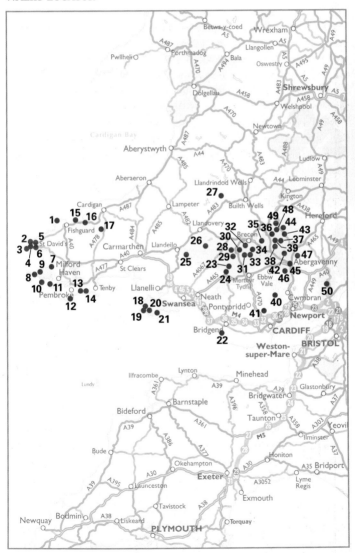

Walking in Brecon Beacons & South Wales

There is no specific line on a map and there is no archetypal landscape or terrain that defines South Wales. More than anything, South Wales defines itself by its variety and its contrasts. From beach to mountain, cathedral to chapel, villain to saint and common to capital, the only parity is the disparity. The common thread is that they all have their beauties and they will all capture your imagination.

A TALE OF TWO PARKS

The majority of the walks in this book are centred on the area's two National Parks. The Pembrokeshire Coast alone boasts over 180 miles (290km) of coast path, but this doesn't tell half the story. The history, adorned with myths and legends of the saints and kings of Wales fills in some of the gaps, though it still says little about the wildlife. Seabirds, seals and porpoises vie for your attention, while falcons share the flower-carpeted cliff tops with a host of other fascinating creatures.

THE BRECON BEACONS

The central peaks of the Brecon Beacons National Park, or the true 'Brecon Beacons', see the most adulation. As well as boasting the highest ground in southern Britain, their tabletop summits preside over some of the finest upland scenery this country can offer. To the east, the Black Mountains are a hill-walkers paradise; their lumbering whaleback ridges and deeply cloven valleys are riddled with tracks and trails that make exploration both safe and easy. The two westernmost ranges, Fforest Fawr and the Black Mountain (singular), are a very different proposition, composed mainly of huge tracts of moorland which, on the whole, fall slightly outside the domain of this book. We have however, suggested some of the easier options available, including a tour of the incomparable Waterfall Country and a circuit around the formidable crags of the Carmarthen Fan.

THE BEST OF SOUTH WALES

The remainder of the walks showcase other favourite images of South Wales, and cherry-pick the best of the Gower coast, visiting swathes of golden sand embedded in jagged limestone cliffs, and sample a beautiful stretch of the Glamorgan Heritage Coast.

No book on this region would be complete without a mention of the Valleys and, of course, the industries that formed their tightly knit communities. Few landscapes have altered more radically in recent decades and the revitalised hilltops now make for some surprisingly

Right: Birds on Llangorse Lake, Brecon Beacons National Park (Walk 35)

good walking. This book also touches on the capital, Cardiff, making an invigorating tour from a fairy-tale castle, just a few miles from the centre. Finally, the region's boundaries have been stretched as far as possible. To the north, it includes the austere charms of Abergwesyn Common, a definite walk on the wild side and once the last stand of the beautiful red kite. And east, to the border, to follow the lazy line of the meandering River Wye through some stunning deciduous woodland. Every mile of this country is an honour and a privilege to walk across and we hope that you will enjoy discovering the history, beauty and wildlife of this fascinating area.

PUBLIC TRANSPORT   Most of the walks in the book return to their original starting point. Unfortunately, these starting points are often in rural areas where there is little or no public transport. The three linear walks are connected by regular bus services, although this may vary at weekends, bank holidays and in the winter. For public transport details call 0871 200 22 33 and ask for the area you are visiting. Information is also available on the internet at www.traveline-cymru.info.

Above: Sugar Loaf mountain (Walk 42)

Walking in Safety

All these walks are suitable for any reasonably fit person, but less experienced walkers should try the easier walks first. Route finding is usually straightforward, but you will find that an Ordnance Survey or AA walking map is a useful addition to the route maps and descriptions; recommendations can be found in the information panels.

RISKS

Although each walk here has been researched with a view to minimising the risks to the walkers who follow its route, no walk in the countryside can be considered to be completely free from risk. Walking in the outdoors will always require a degree of common sense and judgement to ensure that it is as safe as possible.

- Be particularly careful on cliff paths and in upland terrain, where the consequences of a slip can be very serious.
- Remember to check tidal conditions before walking on the seashore.
- Some sections of route are by, or cross, busy roads. Take care and remember traffic is a danger even on minor country lanes.
- Be careful around farmyard machinery and livestock, especially if you have children with you.
- Be aware of the consequences of changes in the weather and check the forecast before you set out. Carry spare clothing and a torch if you are walking in the winter months. Remember the weather can change very quickly at any time of the year, and in moorland and heathland areas, mist and fog can make route finding much harder. Don't set out in these conditions unless you are confident of your navigation skills in poor visibility. In summer remember to take account of the heat and sun; wear a hat and carry water.
- On walks away from centres of population you should carry a whistle and survival bag. If you do have an accident requiring the emergency services, make a note of your position as accurately as possible and dial 999.

COUNTRYSIDE CODE
- Be safe, plan ahead and follow any signs.
- Leave gates and property as you find them.
- Protect plants and animals and take your litter home.
- Keep dogs under close control.
- Consider other people.

For more information visit www.naturalengland.org.uk/ourwork/enjoying/countrysidecode.

Overleaf: Strumble Head and lighthouse (Walk 1)

Around Strumble Head

DISTANCE 8 miles (12.9km)	MINIMUM TIME 3hrs 30min

ASCENT/GRADIENT 920ft (280m) ▲▲▲   LEVEL OF DIFFICULTY ✦✦✦

PATHS Coastal path, grassy, sometimes muddy tracks, rocky paths

LANDSCAPE Rugged headland, secluded caves and rocky tor

SUGGESTED MAP OS Explorer OL35 North Pembrokeshire

START/FINISH Grid reference: SM894411

DOG FRIENDLINESS Care needed near cliff tops and livestock

PARKING Car park by Strumble Head Lighthouse

PUBLIC TOILETS None on route

This is a wonderful stretch of the Pembrokeshire coast, although at times it feels like 'coast path meets the Himalayas', as the narrow ribbon of trail climbs and drops at regular intervals throughout. This is the real wild side of Pembrokeshire, where the headland cliffs tower above the pounding Atlantic surf, the path cuts an airy, at times precarious, line across their tops and the sky is alive with the sound of seabirds. Atlantic grey seals, porpoises and even dolphins are regularly spotted in the turbulent waters. Garn Fawr, a rocky tor that lords it over the whole peninsula, brings a touch of hill walking to the experience, and the shapely lighthouse flashes a constant reminder of just how treacherous these spectacular waters can be.

BEACON OF LIGHT

Built in 1908 to help protect the ferries that run between Fishguard and Ireland, the Strumble Head Lighthouse guards a hazardous stretch of coast that wrecked at least 60 ships in the 19th century alone. The revolving lights, which flash four times every 15 seconds, were originally controlled by a massive clockwork system that needed rewinding every 12 hours. This was replaced in 1965 by an electrically powered system and the lighthouse was then converted to unstaffed operation in 1980. It's possible to cross the daunting narrow chasm that separates Ynys Meicel (St Michael's Island), where the lighthouse stands, from the mainland by a rickety bridge.

ATLANTIC GREY SEALS

This is one of the best walks on which to spot these marine giants that reach over 8ft (2.4m) in length and weigh as much as 770lbs (350kg). They are usually seen just off the coast, but in autumn, when the females give birth to a single pup, they often haul up on to inaccessible beaches where the young are suckled on milk with a high fat content. The best places to see seals are the bays of Pwll Bach and Pwlluog.

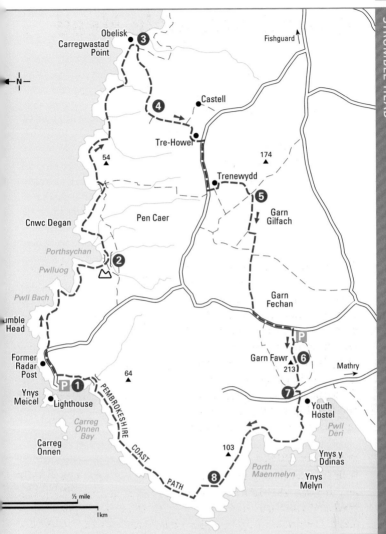

❶ Walk back up the road and cross a gate on the left on to the coast path. Pass above the bays of Pwll Bach and Pwlluog, then drop steeply to a footbridge behind the pebble beach of Porthsychan.

❷ Follow the coast path waymarkers around Cnwc Degan and down to another bridge, where a couple of footpaths lead away from the coast. Continue along the coast, passing a cottage on the right and climbing

and dropping several times, before you reach the obelisk at Carregwastad Point.

❸ Follow the main path inland and turn right then bear left. Continue with this path, which is vague in places, up through the gorse to a wall, then turn right to walk the length of a field to a stile and go on to a good track. Take this through a succession of gates and around a left-hand bend.

4 Ignore a track to the right and continue up the cattle track, eventually bearing right into the farmyard where you follow a walkway past livestock pens before swinging left, after the buildings, to the road. Turn right and follow the road past a large house to a waymarked bridleway on the left. Pass Trenewydd and go through a gate on to a green lane. Follow this up to another gate and on to open ground.

5 Turn right here and follow the wall to yet another gate. This leads to a walled track which you follow to the road. Turn left and climb up to the car park beneath Garn Fawr. Turn right, on to a hedged track, and follow this up, through a gap in the wall, and over rocks to the trig point.

6 Climb down and follow the path to cross the saddle between this tor and the other, slightly lower, one to the south. From here head west towards an even lower outcrop and pass it on the left. Continue on this clear path that leads down to a stile. Cross this and turn left, then right on to a drive that leads to the road.

7 Walk straight across and on to the coast path. Bear right past the youth hostel and cross a stile to drop down towards Ynys y Ddinas, the small island ahead. Navigation is easy as you follow the coast path north, over Porth Maenmelyn and up to a cairn.

8 Continue along the coast, towards the lighthouse, until you return to the car park.

WHERE TO EAT AND DRINK The one down side about walking in such a wild spot is the lack of facilities. There is occasionally an ice-cream van in the car park at the start. Failing that, there's the Farmers Arms in Mathry, further south, or head east towards Fishguard, where there's plenty of choice.

WHAT TO SEE The small hut beneath the car park at the start was a World War II radar post which has been converted into a bird observatory. This is one of the best ornithology spots in the country, particularly well known for spotting migratory birds leaving in autumn and arriving in the spring. As well as obvious seabirds, look out for early swallows and swifts, also large numbers of warblers and other small migrants.

WHILE YOU'RE THERE At Carregwastad Point is a stone obelisk that marks the spot of the last hostile invasion of Britain. On 22 February 1797, a small French force known as the Legion Noire came ashore and set up camp at Tre-Howel, a local farm. The invaders were quick to take advantage of a huge haul of liquor that had been salvaged from a recent wreck and, subsequently unfit to fight, were forced to surrender within two days.

Around St David's Head

DISTANCE 3.5 miles (5.7km)   MINIMUM TIME 2hrs

ASCENT/GRADIENT 425ft (130m) ▲▲▲   LEVEL OF DIFFICULTY ✛✛✛

PATHS Coast path, clear paths across heathland

LANDSCAPE Dramatic cliffs, heather- and gorse-covered hillsides

SUGGESTED MAP OS Explorer OL35 North Pembrokeshire

START/FINISH Grid reference: SM734271

DOG FRIENDLINESS Care needed on cliff tops and near livestock

PARKING Whitesands Beach

PUBLIC TOILETS At start

Steeped in legend, peppered with the evidence of civilisations past, and scenically stunning, it would be difficult to imagine a more atmospheric place than St David's Head. For full effect, visit at sunset and watch the sky turn red over the scattered islets of the Bishops and Clerks.

ST DAVID'S HEAD

Carn Llidi, a towering monolith of ancient rock that has all the attributes of a full-blown mountain, yet stands only 594ft (181m) above sea level, dominates the headland. Its colourful heather- and gorse-covered flanks are alive with small heathland birds, which chatter from the swaying ferns and dart for cover in the hidden crannies of dry-stone walls. The coast, when you meet it, is at its intricate finest; a succession of narrow zawns (clefts), broken up by stubborn headlands that thrust defiantly into the ever-present swells. The Head itself is truly magnificent and a few minutes spent exploring will quickly uncover a series of rocky terraces that offer shelter from the wind and stunning views over the ocean to Ramsey Island.

THE WARRIOR'S DYKE

Despite its hostile demeanour, St David's Head was once home to a thriving Iron Age community who lived in huts and kept their stock in a field system, the remains of which are still visible. The headland, naturally guarded by the ocean on three sides, was also defended by the Clawydd-y-Milwry (the Warrior's Dyke) at its eastern edge. The dyke is actually formed by three ditches and two ramparts that cut across the neck of the headland. The main bastion, a dry-stone wall that would have once stood around 15ft (4.6m) tall, is still easily visible as a linear pile of stones and rocks. Within the fort there are a number of standing stones, stone circles and the remains of basic huts. The defences are thought to have been built around AD 100.

BURIAL CHAMBERS

At least 3,000 years older, but well worth seeking out, is Coetan Arthur, a neolithic quoit, or burial chamber, which stands directly above a narrow zawn, bounded on its eastern walls by the red-coloured crags of Craig Coetan, a popular climbing venue. Coetan Arthur consists of a 12ft (3.7m) long capstone, propped up on a smaller rock. The quoit would have originally been covered with earth to form a mound, but this has long since eroded. There is evidence of several more burial chambers near the summit of Carn Llidi. Happily, both the headland and Carn Llidi are in the care of the National Trust, and you are free to wander at will to investigate these fascinating sites. However, you should bear in mind that they are Scheduled Ancient Monuments and therefore protected by law.

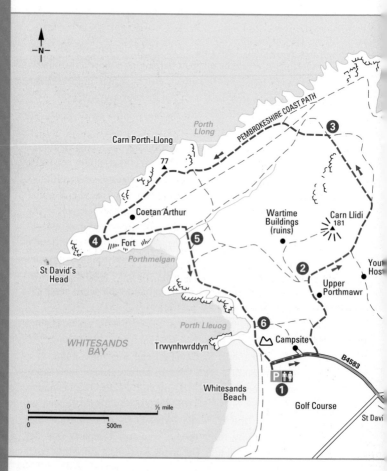

1 From Whitesands Beach head back up the road, pass the caravan site and immediately turn left along a road. Bear right where it splits and continue around a left-hand bend to walk up to the buildings. Keep left to walk between the houses, then carry on to a gate.

2 Turn right shortly afterwards on to the open heathland and follow the footpath along the wall beneath Carn Llidi. Pass the track that drops to the youth hostel on the right and continue, keeping right wherever the track forks. Go over a crest and downhill to a corner of a wall where a clear track runs diagonally left towards the coast.

3 Follow this to the coast path, where there's a small fingerpost, and turn left to walk along the cliff tops. At Porth Llong, the path bears right to climb to a cairn. The headland is a labyrinth of paths and tracks, but for maximum enjoyment try to stick as close to the cliff tops as possible as

you round a number of narrow zawns. The official coast path doesn't go as far as the tip of the peninsula, but plenty of other tracks do, so follow one as far as you wish.

4 From the tip, turn left and make your way through the rocky outcrops on the southern side of the headland. As you approach Porthmelgan you will pick up an obvious path near the cliff tops which you should work your way down to using one of the many small paths.

5 This leads to a small footbridge over a stream which you cross to climb up the steps on the other side. Continue to a kissing gate where the National Trust land ends and maintain your direction. Pass above Porth Lleuog and the distinctive rocky promontory of Trwynhwrddyn, which is worth a visit in its own right.

6 The path then drops steeply down to the road at the entrance to Whitesands Beach.

WHERE TO EAT AND DRINK Apart from a cafe serving light meals, snacks and drinks in the car park, the best place to eat and drink near this walk is St David's itself. The Farmers Arms is the pick of the bunch, boasting a wonderful patio area, which can be a real suntrap on a summer afternoon. For coffee, try Pebbles Yard Gallery Espresso Bar, in the centre.

WHAT TO SEE The small islets west of the headland are the Bishops and Clerks. The northernmost and largest is North Bishop and the southernmost, crowned with a lighthouse, is South Bishop. The others all have individual names but are most often just referred to as the Clerks.

WHILE YOU'RE THERE The views from the rocky crest of Carn Llidi are among the finest on the whole coast – especially delightful at sunset. The easiest ascent is from the western side, where a broad track leads up the ridge past the ruined wartime buildings.

Overleaf: St David's Head at sunset (Walk 2)

The Shores of Ramsey Sound

DISTANCE 3.5 miles (5.7km)		MINIMUM TIME 2hrs	

ASCENT/GRADIENT 197ft (60m) ▲▲▲   LEVEL OF DIFFICULTY ✛✛✛

PATHS Coast path and easy farmland tracks

LANDSCAPE Undulating coast, dramatic views to Ramsey Island

SUGGESTED MAP OS Explorer OL35 North Pembrokeshire

START/FINISH Grid reference: SM724252

DOG FRIENDLINESS One dog-proof stile and farmyard

PARKING Car park above lifeboat station at St Justinian's

PUBLIC TOILETS Nearest at Porth Clais or Whitesands

This is one of the easiest walks, but it's also one of the most rewarding, with drop-dead gorgeous coastal scenery and plenty of chances to spot some of Pembrokeshire's varied wildlife. On a calm summer's day, the bobbing boats in Ramsey Sound display the kind of tranquillity you'd usually associate with a Greek island. See it on a rough day, with a spring tide running, and the frothing, seething currents that whip through the narrow channel are frightening to say the least. If the views aren't enough, a keen eye and a handy pair of binoculars may well produce sightings of seals, porpoises, dolphins, choughs and even peregrine falcons.

ST JUSTINIAN

St Justinian was a hermit from Brittany who became the abbot of St David's Cathedral and acted as St David's confessor. Disillusioned with the lethargic attitude of the monks, he absconded to Ramsey Island to establish a more spiritual community. Some of his more loyal monks travelled with him, but eventually even they became fed up with his strict regimes and chopped off his head. It is said he walked back across Ramsey Sound carrying it in his arms. His remains were buried in the small chapel on the hillside overlooking the sound, which bears his name. Later St David took them to his own church. St Justinian is revered as a martyr, his assassins are thought to have been under demonic influence, and his life is celebrated on 5 December each year.

RAMSEY ISLAND

Less than 2 miles (3.2km) long and 446ft (136m) high at its tallest point, Ramsey Island is a lumbering humpback ridge separated from the St David's coast by a narrow sound. Known in Welsh as Ynys Ddewi (St David's Isle), this is the place where, legend suggests, St David met

St Patrick. It's a haven for wildlife and has belonged to the RSPB as a nature reserve since 1992. The eastern coast looks pretty tame, but the western seaboard boasts some of Pembrokeshire's tallest and most impressive cliffs, punctuated with sea caves and rock arches that are the breeding grounds of the area's largest seal colony. At its narrowest point, a string of jagged rocks known as The Bitches protrude into the sound. Tides gush through them at speeds of up to 8 knots, creating a playground for white-water kayakers. Looking out of place against the ocean backdrop, the island is populated by a herd of red deer.

HARBOUR PORPOISES

Ramsey Sound is a great place to spot harbour porpoises. Resembling dolphins, though never more than 7ft (2.1m) in length, small schools of these cetaceans crop up all around the coast, but are often seen feeding in the currents at either end of the sound. Unlike dolphins, they seldom leap from the water, but on a calm day their arched backs and small dorsal fins are easy to spot if you scan the ocean from a promontory like Pen Dal-Aderyn with a pair of binoculars.

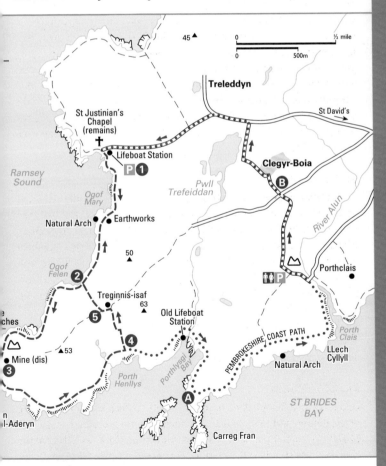

1 Walk down to the lifeboat station and turn left on to the coast path, above the steps. Follow this, passing above a number of lofty, grassy promontories that make great picnic spots. After 0.5 miles (800m), look out for the traces of Iron Age earthworks on the left.

2 Pass a gate and a track on your left – this is your return route – and swing around to the west above Ogof Felen. This is a good seal pup beach in autumn. The trail climbs slightly and then drops steeply to a ruined copper mine, directly opposite The Bitches.

3 Continue easily to Pen Dal-Aderyn and then swing eastwards to enter St Brides Bay. The path climbs above some magnificent cliffs and passes between a few rocky outcrops before veering north above the broad bay

of Porth Henllys. Drop down into a shallow valley until you come to a fingerpost at a junction of paths.

4 Turn left up four very short flights of steps and past a pink cottage to walk away from the coast and then cross a stile on the right, into a field. Turn left to follow the track along the wall to a gate and stile, where you enter a courtyard. Turn left here at a fingerpost pointing to Porthstinian. About 20yds (18m) before you reach a metal farm gate with a walkers' gate beside it, swing right and walk to a clear track.

5 Follow this track down between dry-stone walls to reach another gate, which leads back out on to the coast path. Turn right and retrace your outward route along the grassy clifftop path back to St Justinian's.

WHERE TO EAT AND DRINK There are plenty of options in St David's, but the Pebbles Yard Gallery Espresso Bar in the centre is probably the best bet for great coffee and freshly prepared food. For pub grub and a drink, the Farmers Arms in Goat Street is a good choice.

WHAT TO SEE Take a second look at any of the small crows you see as you follow this stretch of coast path. What appears at first glance to be a jackdaw is probably sporting a sharp red bill and bright red legs and is one of Britain's rarest crows, the chough. These small birds are incredibly common in Pembrokeshire, however, where they nest on ledges and feed mainly on insects.

WHILE YOU'RE THERE Take a boat trip around Ramsey Island. As well as getting a close-up look at the seal colonies on the western flanks, you'll also get a great view of the rushing waters of The Bitches. Wear waterproofs as it can get pretty wet.

Ramsey Sound to Porth Clais

DISTANCE 7 miles (11.3km)   MINIMUM TIME 3hrs

ASCENT/GRADIENT 425ft (130m) ▲▲▲   LEVEL OF DIFFICULTY ✦✦✦

SEE MAP AND INFORMATION PANEL FOR WALK 3

For most of the year, this extended walk starts at St Justinian's and you will need to follow the quiet lanes from Porth Clais to finish. In summer, however, it's possible to begin in St David's and take the Celtic Coaster hourly bus service to St Justinian's, then catch it back again from Porth Clais at the end.

Whichever way you chose, follow Walk 3 to Point ❹ and stay on the coast path to climb up out of the dip. This leads around Maen Llwydwyn and down to Porthlysgi Bay. This was the site of the original St David's lifeboat station, replaced by the one you passed at St Justinian's. Cross a stream as it runs down the beach and turn left to climb back up, behind the beach, and on to the cliff tops (Point ❹) near the rocky island of Carreg Fran. The gradient eases again and the path now cruises comfortably along a wonderful section of coast, studded with rock arches and caves. At Llech Cyllyll, turn back inland to drop down into the deeply cloven inlet of Porth Clais.

The harbour was built in the 12th century and was once the main port for St David's, used for importing coal and timber among other things. The main car park is on the site of the now defunct St David's gasworks. These in turn had been built over the site of a spring, said to be the place that St David was baptised. Porth Clais is also purported to be the landing place of the legendary magic boar, Twrch Trywyth, after he swam from Ireland to confront King Arthur.

Turn left on to the road and climb steeply past the car park. Continue easily to a crossroads and keep straight ahead to pass Clegyr-Boia (Point ❸) and the small lake of Pwll Trefeiddan, a popular stop-over for migrating waterfowl. Turn left at the T-junction and follow the road back to St Justinian's, ignoring the turning to the right.

WHAT TO LOOK OUT FOR St David's lifeboat station was built in 1911 and replaced the original station situated in Porthlysgi Bay. The current boat is called the *Garside* and was commissioned on 25 May 1988. The station was used to make the ITV drama series *Lifeboat* in the early 1990s when Ramsey Island took on the name of Pendragon Island.

The Northern Reaches of St Brides Bay

DISTANCE 9 miles (14.5km)	MINIMUM TIME 4hrs
ASCENT/GRADIENT 1,280ft (390m) ▲▲▲	LEVEL OF DIFFICULTY ✦✦✦

PATHS Coast path

LANDSCAPE High cliffs and sheltered coves

SUGGESTED MAP OS Explorer OL35 North Pembrokeshire

START Grid reference: SM757252   FINISH Grid reference: SM847224

DOG FRIENDLINESS Care needed near cliff edges

PARKING Pay-and-display car park in St David's

PUBLIC TOILETS By tourist information centre at start and at Solva harbour

While circular walks are a means to an end, coastal path connoisseurs prefer linear routes, as there's no need to dilute the quality of the coastal section with often less interesting terrain. The key to success is public transport and fortunately a few stretches of the Pembrokeshire Coast Path link well with buses – the county now boasts six separate services shuttling around the coast – to allow some of the finest walks to be completed without compromise. This section, along the northern reaches of St Brides Bay, is one of the best.

SOLVA

Halfway along the walk lies Solva, a village divided into the larger Upper Solva and the more picturesque Lower Solva down by the harbour. It was this harbour that gave Solva its *raison d'être* and in the Middle Ages the village became a hub for trading in the St Brides Bay area. Solva's well-preserved lime kilns are testament to the harbour's importance as a dropping-off point for limestone, which would be heated to produce lime. This would then be spread over the fields to increase fertility. Wool and woollen produce were also traded at the harbour. Indeed, Solva Woollen Mill, a short distance from the village at Middle Hill, is the oldest continuously working woollen mill in Pembrokeshire. Moved from St David's to its present location in 1907, it was equipped with a 10ft waterwheel and all the machinery necessary to turn fleeces into useable fabric. The wheel powered a number of looms but there was also a hand loom on site which was used for weaving stair-carpet. The mill has been restored in recent years and makes for a fine detour.

If you want to turn your walk into a mini adventure you can take a two-hour cruise on the MV *Swift* from Solva harbour to seek out the delights of the north side of St Brides Bay right up to Ramsey Sound.

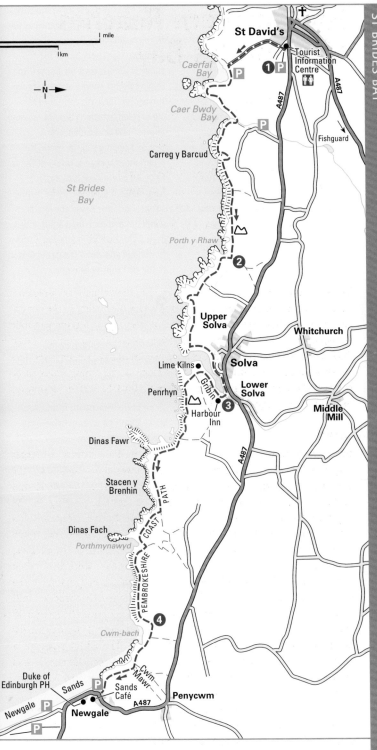

1 mile

1 km

—N→

St David's

✝

Caerfai Bay

Tourist Information Centre

🅿 ➊ 🅿 ℹ

A487

Caer Bwdy Bay

🅿

Fishguard

Carreg y Barcud

St Brides Bay

Porth y Rhaw

➋

Upper Solva

Whitchurch

Lime Kilns ●

Solva

Penrhyn

Gribin

Lower Solva

Middle Mill

➌

Harbour Inn

Dinas Fawr

A487

Stacen y Brenhin

COAST PATH

Dinas Fach

Porthmynawyd

PEMBROKESHIRE

➍

Cwm-bach

Duke of Edinburgh PH

Cwm Mawr

Sands

🅿

Sands Café

Penycwm

Newgale

🅿

A487

Newgale

🅿

❶ Turn left out of the car park in St David's and walk down the road towards Caerfai Bay. You'll meet the coast path on the left-hand side of a small car park. Follow it down, ignoring a right turn to the beach, and bear south to round a broad promontory, tipped with a rocky bluff. The path swings left and drops down to Caer Bwdy Bay, where you'll pass a ruined mill on the left. Climb back up on to the cliff tops to continue above Carreg y Barcud and around another inlet. The next section slips by easily, above a series of caves and arches, before you drop steeply down to Porth y Rhaw.

❷ Climb out again and enjoy huge views over more cliffs and bluffs. One mile (1.6km) after Porth y Rhaw you'll be drawn back inland as the path dips into the sharp gash of Solva. Go through a gate and follow the the field edge down to another gate, where you turn right. This leads on to a narrow track. Follow this down and then around to the left. Continue beneath houses before dropping down a waymarked path on the right that leads down steps to the harbour. Follow the harbour wall along to the Harbour Inn and Thirty Five cafe.

❸ Cross the bridge and turn left and then right to rejoin the coast path. After taking a right fork to pass above some fantastically well-preserved lime kilns, follow the path up on to the ridge of Gribin. The names Gribin or Cribin, literally translate to 'ridge'. At the seaward end you'll pass the banks of an Iron Age settlement. Turn left at a waymarker to drop steeply down steps to a footbridge in the valley

below. Cross the pebbles at the back of the beach and climb steeply up on to the headland of Penrhyn. Don't be drawn right here but at the top turn left almost back on yourself to rejoin the cliff edge, a short distance further on. The path continues to climb steadily from this point, passing above a few beautiful beaches before dropping slightly above the pronounced rocky peninsula of Dinas Fawr. An airy scramble along its back makes a great excursion if time allows. Continue easily above Stacen y Brenhin and then drop again into a deep valley by Porthmynawyd. Cross a footbridge and climb the path back on to the cliff tops once more.

❹ The wide sweeping sands of Newgale are now visible ahead and, as you are drawn back inland at Cwm-bach, you should be able to see if the tide is low enough to allow you to finish the walk on the beach itself or whether you'll need to climb back up on to the coast path from Cwm Mawr. Climb away from Cwm-bach and then, almost immediately, drop into Cwm Mawr. The beach is accessed by a short scramble down rocks on the right. If the tide's out, continue easily along the beach, past a number of huge caves, to Newgale. Once on Newgale Beach, keep the cliffs to your left and walk up to the huge pebble bank above. Scale this and cross behind the small stream to gain the road. If the tide's too high, climb away from Cwm Mawr and continue along the coast path, with fantastic views west along the coast. This leads out on to the road at Newgale, where you turn right to drop to the village.

A Pilgrimage Around St Non's Bay

DISTANCE 3.5 miles (5.7km)   MINIMUM TIME 1hr 30min

ASCENT/GRADIENT 262ft (80m) ▲▲▲   LEVEL OF DIFFICULTY ✦✦✦

PATHS Coast path and clear footpaths over farmland

LANDSCAPE Leafy countryside and dramatic cliffs

SUGGESTED MAP OS Explorer OL35 North Pembrokeshire

START/FINISH Grid reference: SM757252

DOG FRIENDLINESS On lead around St Non's Chapel and St Non's Well

PARKING Pay-and-display car park in St David's

PUBLIC TOILETS Next to tourist information centre

This walk makes a great evening stroll. The paths that lead from the city are pleasant and easy to follow but as always they're quickly forgotten as you step out into the more glamorous surroundings of the coast. The all-too-short section of towering buttresses and jagged islets leads easily to a spot that can claim to be the very heart of spiritual Wales – the birthplace of St David. The serenity of the location soothes the mind in readiness for the short jaunt back to the compact little city he founded.

PATRON SAINT

Considering the immense influence he has had on Welsh culture, little is known about the patron saint himself. His mother is said to be St Non, derived from Nun or Nonita, who was married to a local chieftain called Sant. They settled somewhere near Trwyn Cynddeiriog, the rocky bluff that forms the western walls of the bay named after her. Legend suggests that David was born around AD 500, in the place where the ruined chapel stands today. Although a fierce storm raged throughout his birth, a calm light was said to have lit the scene. By the morning, a fresh spring had erupted nearby, becoming the Holy Well of St Non and visited on this walk. St David went on to be baptised by St Elvis at Porthclais, in water from another miraculous spring.

MAN WITH A MISSION

David would have been well educated and it is believed that he undertook a number of religious odysseys, including one to Jerusalem, before he finally returned to his birthplace around AD 550. He then founded a church and monastery at Glyn Rhosyn, on the banks of the River Alun, on the site of the present cathedral, where he set about trying to spread the Christian word. St David's Day is celebrated on 1 March every year and St Non, who saw out her life in Brittany, is remembered on the day after.

ST DAVID'S CITY

St David's is little more than a pretty village, though it boasts the title 'city' due to its magnificent cathedral. It's a wonderful place and doesn't seem any the worse for the amount of tourism that it attracts. Known as Tyddewi (David's House) in Welsh, the city grew as a result of its coastal position at the western extreme of the British mainland. It would have been linked easily by sea with Ireland and Cornwall. As well as the cathedral and the ruins of the Bishop's Palace, it houses a plethora of gift shops and the National Park information centre, close to the car park, is one of the finest in the country.

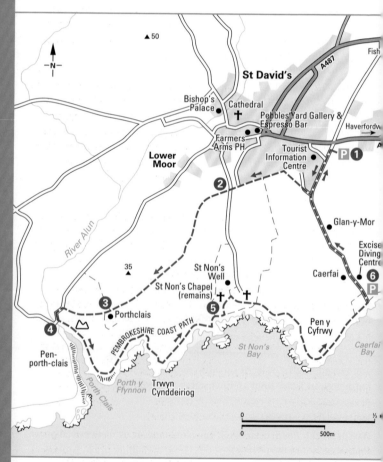

❶ Turn left out of the car park in St David's and walk down the road, as if you were heading for Caerfai

Bay. As the houses thin out, you'll see a turning on the right that leads to more dwellings. Take this turning, and then turn left on to a waymarked bridleway. Follow this bridleway between hedges, past the end of a road and on to reach a junction with another road.

❷ Walk straight across and take the waymarked path to a fork, where you keep right to continue to a gate and, a few places later, a second gate. Continue down a path between gorse hedges to a third gate and carry straight on down the left-hand side of a field to a farmyard.

❸ Go through the gate and turn left towards the farmyard and then right. As the drive swings left, keep straight ahead with the bank to your right. Continue across the next field and drop down between gorse bushes, keeping straight ahead at a crossroads of paths, to the road at Porth Clais. Turn left to the bottom of the valley and then, before crossing the bridge, turn left on to the coast path.

❹ Climb up steeply on to the cliff tops, ignoring the path off to the left at the top, and follow the coast path towards Porth y Ffynnon. The next small headland is Trwyn Cynddeiriog, where there's a lovely grassy platform above the cliffs if you fancy a rest. Continue walking into St Non's Bay and look for a footpath on the left that leads to the ruined chapel.

❺ From the chapel, head up to a gate that leads to St Non's Well and, from there, follow the path beneath the new chapel and straight ahead on to the coast path. Turn left to climb easily on to Pen y Cyfrwy, continue around this and drop down towards Caerfai Bay.

❻ You'll eventually come out beneath the Caerfai Bay car park, where you turn left and climb some steps. Go through the entrance of the car park onto the road, which you then follow back to St David's and the start of the walk.

WHERE TO EAT AND DRINK Apart from the tiny seasonal cafe in the car park at Porth Clais, the best bet for refreshment is St David's where there's plenty of choice. A favourite pub is the Farmers Arms on Goat Street, which has a good garden and serves up all the usual pub fare. For non-alcoholic refreshment, try the excellent Pebbles Yard Gallery Espresso Bar.

WHAT TO SEE Shortly after the stiff climb out of Porth Clais, you'll round Trwyn Cynddeiriog, the headland that divides Porth y Ffynnon from St Non's Bay. This is where St Non and Sant, St David's parents, were said to have lived. A short distance further along the coast path, at the head of the bay, you'll see a footpath on the left that leads to the ruined chapel. This is thought to have been built in the 13th century on the spot where St David was born. A path then leads to a gate, behind which you'll see St Non's Well and a grotto. Further up the hill is the newer chapel, dedicated to Our Lady and St Non. This was actually built in the 1930s using stone from other principle local evangelical sites, including the original chapel.

WHILE YOU'RE THERE St David's Cathedral is both architecturally stunning and spiritually moving. In 1120 Pope Calixtus II decreed that two pilgrimages to St David's were the equivalent of one to Rome – an honour indeed. The cathedral and the nearby Bishop's Palace play host to a series of classical concerts every summer.

Broad Haven and the Haroldston Woods

DISTANCE 3.5 miles (5.7km)   MINIMUM TIME 1hr 30min

ASCENT/GRADIENT 290ft (88m) ▲▲▲   LEVEL OF DIFFICULTY ✦✦✦

PATHS Woodland trail, country lanes and coast path

LANDSCAPE Mixed woodland and lofty cliffs above broad beach

SUGGESTED MAP OS Explorer OL36 South Pembrokeshire

START/FINISH Grid reference: SM863140

DOG FRIENDLINESS Poop scoop around car park and beach. Care needed on cliff tops

PARKING Car park by tourist information centre in Broad Haven

PUBLIC TOILETS Between car park and beach

Woodland walking is something of a rarity along the Pembrokeshire Coast Path, so this short stretch of permissive path, which sneaks through a narrow strip of woodland separating Broad Haven from Haroldston, makes a refreshing diversion from the usual salty air and the cries of the seabirds. This is the easiest of the Pembrokeshire walks in the book, with an almost perfectly level section of coast path, some of which has been surfaced for access by wheelchair users. The artificial path, however, takes nothing away from the quality of the scenery, which is magnificent.

ERODING CLIFFS

The cliffs here are of softer shales and millstone grit making them prone to erosion and subsidence, as you'll witness firsthand along the way. Amazingly, this whole stretch of coast sits on top of huge coal reserves, but the last colliery, which was situated further north in Nolton Haven, actually closed down in the early 1900s. As you progress south you'll pass the crumpled remains of an Iron Age fort on Black Point – although this is rapidly becoming separated from the main cliff by a landslide – and also a diminutive standing stone, known as the Harold Stone, which is tucked away in a field on the left as you approach Broad Haven. It's said to mark the spot where Harold, the Earl of Wessex, defeated the Welsh in the 11th century, but it's actually more likely to be Bronze Age.

COASTAL RESORT

Broad Haven is about as close as you'll get to a traditional seaside resort in North Pembrokeshire. The town's popularity as a holiday destination blossomed in the early 1800s, but recent years have seen an acceleration in development that has resulted in almost wall-to-wall caravan parks and a significant rise in the number of residential properties. The beach is beautiful, with gently sloping sands encased in brooding dark cliffs. As well as the usual selection of family holiday-makers, it's a popular place with windsurfers. This is due partly to a shop and rental centre behind the beach, and because the prevalent southwesterlies that blow across and onshore from the left make it a safe but fun place to play in the sometimes sizeable surf.

ROCK FORMATIONS

At low tide it's possible to walk south along the beach to the charming village of Little Haven. A walk northwards will reveal some fascinating rock formations beneath the headland. These include Den's Door, an impressive double arch in a rugged sea stack; the Sleek Stone, a humpback rock forced into its contorted position by a geological fault; and Shag Rock and Emmet Rock. Contorted layers of rock are also clearly visible in the main cliffs.

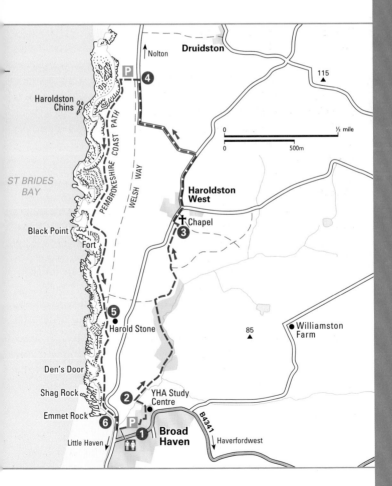

1 From anywhere in the car park, walk towards the youth hostel and follow a waymarked path marked Coedwig Haroldston Woods that runs between the YHA Study Centre (located to the right of the hostel) and the coastguard rescue building. Fork left at the junction with the holiday park path and continue to a gate then a kissing gate, to continue with the stream on your left.

2 Cross the stream by a bridge and now, with the valley floor to your right, go through a gate and bear left to continue easily upwards until you reach a T-junction of paths by a fingerpost. Turn right here, past a part-concealed bench on the right, and then swing left to continue upwards towards another junction of paths by a small chapel.

3 Turn left to the road and then right on to it to walk uphill, with the church on your right. Ignore the turning to the right, then take the first left, towards Druidston Haven. Follow

this past an ineffectual cattle grid to a sharp right-hand bend. Continue for another 300yds (274m) to the Haroldston Chins parking area and a gate on the left.

4 Go through the gate and follow the well-surfaced track down towards the coast. On reaching the cliff tops, bear around to the left and continue past Black Point.

5 After passing the Harold Stone, situated in front of a modern white house on your left, fork right through a gate to remain on the coast path (marked with an acorn). The path starts to drop, generally quite easily, but there is one steep step. Follow the path down to meet the road and turn right.

6 Cross over the bridge and then, just before the road you are on merges into the main road, turn left on to a tarmac footpath that leads through a green and back to the car park.

WHERE TO EAT AND DRINK There's plenty of choice, including pubs, cafes and chip shops in Broad Haven, but the top place for atmosphere, food and setting has to be the Swan on the tiny harbourside in Little Haven. It's an intimate little pub ideal for lunch, dinner or just a pint on the sea wall.

WHAT TO SEE As you turn the sharp right-hand bend on the road at Point **3** you'll see a good track running parallel to the road in the field on your left. This is an ancient trade route, known as the Welsh Way, that runs from Monk's Haven – more commonly known as St Ishmael's – to Whitesands Beach. It was considered a safer mode of transport than sailing across the waters of the bay.

WHILE YOU'RE THERE For a memorable sunset experience, head a few miles north to the tiny beach at Nolton Haven, where you can enjoy the fading daylight in a truly atmospheric setting. A short walk north along the coast path from the beach leads to the distinctive pillar of Rickets Head, which is also easily visible from the beach at Newgale.

Island views from the Marloes Peninsula

DISTANCE 6 miles (9.7km)   MINIMUM TIME 2hrs 30min

ASCENT/GRADIENT 420ft (128m) ▲▲▲   LEVEL OF DIFFICULTY ✦✦✦

PATHS Coast path and clear footpaths, short section on tarmac

LANDSCAPE Rugged cliff tops and beautiful sandy beaches

SUGGESTED MAP OS Explorer OL36 South Pembrokeshire

START/FINISH Grid reference: SM761089

DOG FRIENDLINESS Care near cliff tops and poop scoop on beaches

PARKING National Trust car park above Martin's Haven, near Marloes village

PUBLIC TOILETS Marloes village

The Marloes Peninsula forms the westernmost tip of the southern shores of St Brides Bay. The paddle-shaped headland is a popular place to walk due to the narrow neck that affords minimum inland walking for maximum time spent on the coast. It is famous for its stunning scenery, which includes two of the Pembrokeshire Coast National Park's finest and least-crowded beaches, some secluded coves that are often inhabited by seals, and wonderfully rugged coastline. There are also fine views over a narrow but turbulent sound to the small islands of Skomer and Skokholm – two significant seabird breeding grounds. The walking is captivating, even by Pembrokeshire standards.

WILDLIFE SANCTUARY

Skomer is the largest of the Pembrokeshire islands and is one of the most significant wildlife habitats in the country. In the care of the Wildlife Trust of South and West Wales, the island, separated from the mainland by the rushing waters of Jack Sound, measures approximately 1.5 miles (2.4km) from north to south and 2 miles (3.2km) from east to west. It was declared a National Nature Reserve in 1959 and, as well as the protection it receives as part of the National Park, it's also designated as a Site of Special Scientific Interest (SSSI), a Special Protection Area (SPA) and a Geological Conservation Review Site (GCR). Much of the land is a Scheduled Ancient Monument, courtesy of a number of clearly visible Iron Age settlements and enclosures. If that's not enough of an accolade, the sea that surrounds the island is a Marine Nature Reserve, one of only two in the United Kingdom (the other is Lundy).

The two stars of Skomer are the diminutive but colourful puffin and the dowdy and secretive Manx shearwater. Puffins need little introduction; their colourful beaks and clown-like facial markings put them high on everybody's list of favourite birds. There are around

6,000 nesting pairs on Skomer. They arrive in April and lay a single egg in a burrow. The chick hatches at the end of May and the adult birds spend the next two months ferrying back catches of sand eels for their flightless offspring. After around seven weeks of this lavish attention, the chick leaves the nest, usually at night, and makes its way to the sea.

BASHFUL BIRDS

The mouse-like shearwater is slightly larger than the puffin but it also lays its single egg in a burrow, overlooking the sea. There are around 150,000 pairs on Skomer, Skokholm and Middleholm; which amounts to about 60 per cent of the world's total population. A careful seawatch at last light may reveal them gathering in huge rafts just offshore or even endless lines of flying birds returning to the island – against the sunset, it's quite a magical sight.

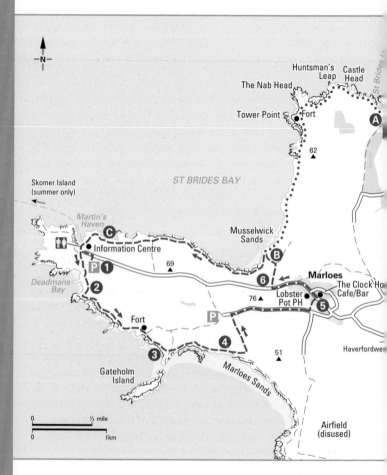

1 From the bottom of the car park, walk down to the bottom of the hill. Bear around to the left, then go through the gate straight ahead into the Deer Park. Turn left and follow the path along to a gate and out on to the coast.

2 With the sea to your right, continue easily along over Deadmans Bay. The next section cruises along easily, passing the earthworks of an Iron Age fort on the left as you approach Gateholm Island.

3 It is possible to get across to the island at low tide, but care is needed to scramble over the slippery rocks. To continue the walk, follow the coast path, above the western end of the beautiful Marloes Sands until you drop almost onto the beach. Turn left to walk along the wide, well-made gravel path.

4 Climb up to the road and turn right here. Follow the road along for around 0.75 miles (1.2km) until you reach a hedged bridleway on the left. Follow this down and emerge by the clock tower.

5 Turn left and pass The Clock House cafe/bar and the Lobster Pot, continuing ahead to leave the village. Ignore a few tracks on the right, as the road bends around to the left, and continue out into open countryside where you'll meet a footpath on the right.

6 Walk down the edge of the field and bear around to the left to drop back down on to the coast path above Musselwick Sands. Turn left and follow the path west for over 1.5 miles (2.4km) to Martin's Haven. Meet the road and climb past the information centre to arrive back at the car park.

WHERE TO EAT AND DRINK The Lobster Pot in Marloes is conveniently placed at the halfway point of the walk, but no dogs or muddy boots, please. The route also takes you right past The Clock House cafe/bar in Marloes which would make for an excellent halfway break.

WHAT TO SEE If you're walking along the coast in spring or summer you'll not fail to be impressed by the small white and pink flowers that carpet the cliff tops. These are sea campion (white) and thrift (pink), both common along the Pembrokeshire coast. As you approach Musselwick Sands, you should be able to see a small island some 8 miles (12.9km) offshore. This is Grassholm and during the summer months it appears almost pure white. It isn't due to the colour of the rock but 30,000 breeding pairs of gannets that return to the island every year. Unlike the puffins and shearwaters of Skomer, the gannets are easily spotted, usually in small flocks, cruising a few hundred yards out looking for fish. If you spot them, watch closely and you'll probably witness their spectacular dive as they fold in their wings and plummet like darts into the water.

WHILE YOU'RE THERE If you have a day to spare then Skomer Island is well worth a visit. The *Dale Princess*, a 50-seat passenger boat, departs Martin's Haven regularly every morning during summer and returns during the afternoon. As well as the wildlife and the relics of ancient civilisations, there's also some fine walking. Note that dogs are not allowed on the island.

Overleaf: St Brides Haven overlooking St Brides Bay (Walks 8 and 9)

St Brides Haven and the Marloes Peninsula

DISTANCE 10 miles (16.1km)   **MINIMUM TIME** 4hrs 30min

ASCENT/GRADIENT 820ft (250m) ▲▲▲   **LEVEL OF DIFFICULTY** +++

START/FINISH Grid Reference: SM802108

PARKING In front of church in St Brides Haven

SEE MAP AND INFORMATION PANEL FOR WALK 8

This walk extends the easy saunter around the peninsula described in Walk 8 by starting at St Brides Haven and following the coast path to Musselwick Sands, where the two walks merge.

St Brides boasts a sheltered, secluded bay, which makes a great spot for a peaceful afternoon on the beach, and the coast path walking from here to Musselwick is both exceptionally pretty and unusually flat, providing plenty of interest for minimum effort. Although it's possible to make this extension into a true circuit by following footpaths north from Marloes village, the coast path is far more interesting.

From the small car park take the path that runs directly in front of the church (Point **Ⓐ**) down to a gap in a wall. Continue past several picnic tables to pick up the coast path as it climbs along the edge of a field towards Castle Head. A gate leads out of the field on to the cliff tops that are then followed steadily upwards to Huntsman's Leap, a narrow cleft in the headland. The path then tracks southwest towards The Nab Head where it finally heads south.

Shortly after this, you'll go through gaps in two walls to pass the earthworks of an Iron Age fort.

The next section is straightforward with no navigation to think about. Continue down into a dip and back up some steps to enjoy the views south to Skomer and Grassholm. Eventually, you'll pass above the broad expanse of beach that makes up Musselwick Sands. Drop into a steep sided dip. Ignore the small path that takes a short cut off to the right and climb to a T-junction where you turn right, almost back on yourself, to continue along the coast path. Here you join Walk 8 at Point **Ⓑ**.

Stay on the Coast Path to follow the instruction for Point **❻** westwards to Point **Ⓒ**, at Martin's Haven. As you reach the road, stay on the coast path and pass through the gate in the wall, to follow Points **❶** to **❺**. These lead you to Marloes Sands, through Marloes and, on the first part of Point **❻**, back to Point **Ⓑ**, where you turn right to retrace your steps to St Brides Haven.

A Circuit of St Ann's Head

DISTANCE 6 miles (9.7km)   MINIMUM TIME 3hrs

ASCENT/GRADIENT 590ft (180m) ▲▲▲   LEVEL OF DIFFICULTY +++

PATHS Coast path, clear paths across farmland

LANDSCAPE Dramatic coastline and entrance to Milford Haven

SUGGESTED MAP OS Explorer OL36 South Pembrokeshire

START/FINISH Grid reference: SM811058

DOG FRIENDLINESS Care needed near livestock

PARKING Large car park next to beach in Dale

PUBLIC TOILETS At start

Despite its beauty and excellence as a walking venue, St Ann's Head is most famous for a sombre tale of incompetence.

The precarious balance between the region's oil refinery and the fragile ecosystems of some of Britain's finest coastline was destroyed on 15 February 1996, when the *Sea Empress* oil tanker grounded on rocks just off St Ann's Head. The collision wasn't particularly bad and because it had taken place near low tide, the ship could have been quickly recovered had the right systems been in place. Tragically, the recovery became a comedy of errors. Numerous salvage propositions were refused and, though the fated ship still had working engines, at one stage she was allegedly denied permission to continue into port under her own steam. By the Sunday evening she was still stranded, having lost only 2,000 tonnes of her cargo. High winds and strong tides continued to batter her against the rocks and finally, six days after she first grounded, she limped into the Haven having spilt at least 72,000 tonnes. The effects were catastrophic: huge oil slicks hit 175 miles (280km) of coastline, including the National Park, 35 Sites of Special Scientific Interest and a National Maritime Nature Reserve.

The immediate victims were the birds: 6,900 were recovered either dead or rescued, but it is estimated that over 20,000 died. The species worst hit was a small black duck known as the common scoter. The damage to fish stocks and other marine life will take years to gauge accurately. The tourist industry was temporarily devastated and the full effect on fishing and related trades won't be known for some time.

Since the disaster, a number of measures have been implemented that should reduce the chances of the same thing happening again. These include better training for pilots, more information on tides, and also the deployment of four very high powered tugs known as

Emergency Towing Vessels at strategic places around the UK coast (Fair Isle, Stornoway, Falmouth and Dover).

The one course of action that won't be undertaken to avoid the repeat of such a disaster is the building of a lighthouse off St Ann's Head. That's because there already is one. The original lighthouse here was built in 1714 while the current one first shed a light on the seas in 1841. This route takes you right past it and the row of cottages that once used to house the lighthouse keepers and their families.

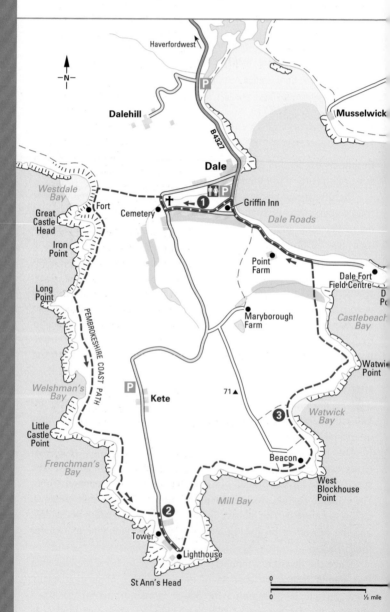

1 Walk back onto the sea front and turn right and then bear right along the road, to head away from the water and between houses. Continue to a T-junction where you turn right, and then as the road bends right again, bear left, through a gate on to a track. As the track bears left, keep ahead and follow the footpath up through a field to a gate that leads on to the coast path above the quiet surfing beach of Westdale Bay. Turn left and climb the steps up on to Great Castle Head, occupied by an Iron Age fort. For the next 2 miles (3.2km), continue along the coast path with the sea to your right and farmland to your left. Despite the spectacular scenery, there are no real drops or climbs and no real opportunities to get lost. Relax and enjoy the ambience until you arrive at the Coastguard Headquarters on St Ann's Head.

2 When you meet the road, turn right and walk along the drive, past the lookout tower, to a gate. Here, the coast path veers left and then immediately right, to follow a series of marker posts along a fence towards the lighthouse and a bank of cottages on the right. At the cottages, bear left then turn sharp left to cross the green to a track that leads behind a walled enclosure. This then drops to join the coast again above Mill Bay, where a plaque gives details of the landing of the exiled Henry Tudor, Earl of Richmond, in 1485, on his way to the Battle of Bosworth. Descend to cross the head of the bay and climb up again to follow field edges around to the beacon on West Blockhouse Point. You'll then come to a crossroads, where you keep straight ahead.

3 The path continues to follow the coast, passing the finest of the beaches along this stretch, Watwick Bay. Continue away from the beach and follow the path, both on cliff tops and field edges, and past a dew pond, to the beacon on Watwick Point. After running along the edge of another two fields, you start the descent to Castlebeach Bay. Cross the footbridge and climb up steps towards the narrow peninsula of Dale Point. As the ground levels, you'll meet a junction of paths where you keep straight ahead to the road. Turn left and follow it down, through woodland, to Dale and the car park.

WHERE TO EAT AND DRINK The waterfront Griffin Inn in Dale is a local institution usually bustling with sailors, surfers, divers and a host of other outdoor enthusiasts. The food and drink are as good as the atmosphere. There are also a couple of tea shops in the village.

WHAT TO SEE The blockhouses and fort along this stretch of coast show how much strategic military importance was placed on Milford Haven in the past. West Blockhouse, above Watwick Bay, was built in 1857 for a garrison of 80 men. Dale Fort, now a field study centre and seen towards the end of the walk, was also built in the 1850s and would have been garrisoned by a similar number of men. The beacons that dominate the headlands now are part of a complex series of waymarkers that aid tankers into the Haven.

Around Milford Haven

DISTANCE 9 miles (14.5km)	MINIMUM TIME 4hrs

ASCENT/GRADIENT 1,017ft (310m) ▲▲▲   LEVEL OF DIFFICULTY +++

PATHS Coast path and easy tracks over agricultural land, short road section

LANDSCAPE Rugged coastline, magnificent beach and sheltered harbour

SUGGESTED MAP OS Explorer OL36 South Pembrokeshire

START/FINISH Grid reference: SM854031

DOG FRIENDLINESS Care needed on cliff tops and near livestock

PARKING Car park at West Angle Bay

PUBLIC TOILETS At start and just off route in Angle village

The narrow finger of land that juts out between Freshwater West and Angle Bay forms the eastern wall of the mouth of Milford Haven. On the northern edge of the peninsula, the waters are passive, lapping against a coastline that's gentle and sloping, but as you round the headland, a radical transformation takes place. Here, the cliffs stand tall and proud, defiantly resisting the full brunt of the considerable Atlantic swells. There are other differences too. While the views along the seaward coast are wild and unspoilt, the inner shores of the Haven reveal the ugly scars of industry; smoking oil refinery chimneys dominate the eastern skyline. The narrow shape of the peninsula lends itself to a challenging circular walk that shows both sides of the coin. The outward leg, as far as Freshwater West, is as tough as coast path walking gets; dipping and climbing on narrow, often quite exposed, paths. The return leg is more civilised, tracking easily around curved Angle Bay and following field-edges back out on to the headland.

Milford Haven is the name of both a huge natural inlet, once described by Admiral Nelson as 'the finest port in Christendom', and the small town that nestles on its northern shores. Despite the obvious advantages of the sheltered waterways, the Haven saw only limited development until the 20th century. The town and dock sprang up in the late 1700s to house a small whaling community that had fled from Nantucket, Massachusetts, during the American War of Independence.

LIFELINES AND CONTROVERSY

Large-scale fishing in the rich waters of the Pembrokeshire coast threw the port a lifeline in the early 1900s and then, as this too declined, mainly due to over-fishing, energy production took over as the area's main industry. There were once three refineries and a power station at the head of the Haven. An LNG (Liquid Natural Gas) terminal was built at Milford a few years ago, while September 2012 saw the opening of Pembroke B, the largest gas-fired power station in Europe.

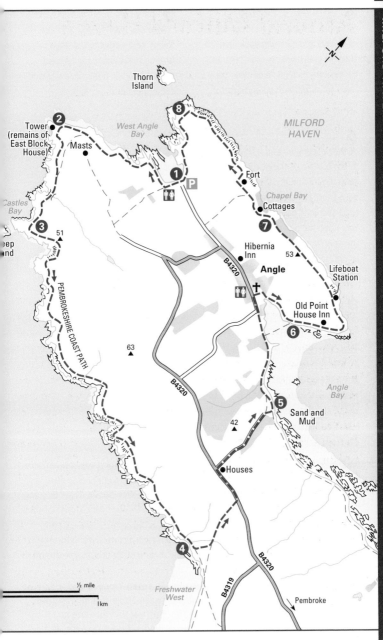

1 Facing the sea, walk left out of the car park and pass between the derelict cafe and the public conveniences to a waymarked gate. Follow the field-edge along, passing through further gates, and eventually leading out on to the coast, where a right fork drops down towards a ruined tower on a slender headland.

2 Continue back up, pass through further gates, then go down to a tiny footbridge. Climb up from this and pass Sheep Island on your right.

3 Continue along the coast, dropping steeply into a succession of valleys and climbing back up each time. As you reach the northern end of Freshwater West, keep your eye open for a footpath waymarker to the left.

4 Cross a stile and walk up the floor of the valley, swinging left to a stile at the top. Cross the next field, to a kissing gate and another field to a stile. Cross this and turn left on to the road and walk past a cluster of houses to a right-hand turn. Follow this all the way down to the coast and turn left on to the coast path to merge on to a drive.

5 Take the drive to a bridleway sign on the right. If the tide is low, you can cross the estuary here and continue along the bank of pebbles to the road on the other side. If it's not, carry on along the drive to join a road that leads into Angle village and turn right by the church to follow a gravel track over a bridge and around to the right.

6 Continue around, pass the Old Point House Inn on your left and follow field-edges to the gravel turning point above the lifeboat station on your right. Keep straight ahead and continue walking through a succession of fields into a wooded area.

7 You'll join a broad track that runs around Chapel Bay cottages and fort. Keep straight ahead to follow the narrow path back above the coast. This eventually rounds the headland looking out to Thorn Island.

8 As you descend into West Angle Bay, the path diverts briefly into a field to avoid a landslide. Continue downwards and bear right on to a drive that drops you back to the car park.

WHERE TO EAT AND DRINK The Hibernia Inn in Angle village is conveniently placed for lunch or a drink, but you'd do even better to hold on for the stunningly positioned Old Point House Inn, as you climb above Angle Bay and back out on to the headland.

WHAT TO SEE Milford Haven's potential vulnerability to invasion has led to considerable defences being constructed around its entrance. The stone blockhouse on Thorn Island, now a hotel, is testament to this, as are the other fortifications on St Ann's Head.

WHILE YOU'RE THERE Take a drive or, better still, a walk across the magnificent Cleddau toll bridge that spans the estuary between Neyland and Pembroke Dock. The sweeping curve of the lofty 1970s construction provides stunning views over the whole haven and the coast beyond. It also makes the best connection between North and South Pembrokeshire. To get there follow the A477 from Pembroke.

Beaches and Lakes at Stackpole

DISTANCE 6 miles (9.7km)	MINIMUM TIME 2hrs 30min

ASCENT/GRADIENT 390ft (119m) ▲▲▲   LEVEL OF DIFFICULTY ✦✦✦

PATHS Easy coast path, quiet lanes and well-trodden waterside walkways

LANDSCAPE Magnificent limestone headlands, secluded beaches and tranquil waterways

SUGGESTED MAP OS Explorer OL36 South Pembrokeshire

START/FINISH Grid reference: SR976938

DOG FRIENDLINESS Care needed on cliff tops and near livestock

PARKING National Trust car park above Broad Haven Beach

PUBLIC TOILETS At start and at Stackpole Quay

Together, the limestone headlands of St Govan's and Stackpole create some of the most impressive coastline in South Pembrokeshire. The cliffs, however, make up only a short section of a varied walk that crosses two of the region's finest beaches and also explores some beautiful inland waters. Broad Haven is often referred to as Broad Haven South, to avoid confusion with the town and beach of the same name in St Brides Bay. The beach here is a broad gem of white sand, backed by rolling dunes. Barafundle Bay is equally picturesque, and lack of road access keeps it relatively unspoilt. The final attraction of this simple circuit is the three-fingered waterway that probes deeply inland from Broad Haven. The wooded shores and calm waters make a refreshing change from the wildness of the coast.

The cliffs between Linney Head (closed to the public as part of the MOD firing range) and Stackpole Head comprise some of the best limestone coastal scenery in Britain. Exposed to the full force of the Atlantic, they contain many caves and blowholes. A few spectacular sea stacks stud the coast a short distance offshore – Church Rock, seen on this walk, just off Broad Haven Beach, is one of the finest examples.

BOSHERSTON LILY PONDS

This series of interconnecting lakes was created at the turn of the 19th century by Baron Cawdor, once the owner of the Stackpole Estate. Subsequent drifting of sand has created a large, marram grass-covered dune system behind the beach. The lakes are rich in wildlife, with herons prowling the shallows, swans, ducks, moorhens and coots all visible on the surface, and shyer creatures such as kingfishers often spotted. The lilies are at their best in June, while the woodland is magnificent in spring and autumn.

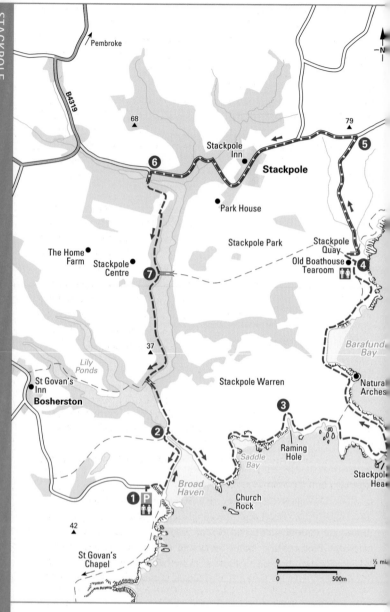

❶ From the car park, head back to the National Trust building at the head of the lane and bear right, down a tarmac path and a set of steps, to the beach. Cross the beach and keep left to walk up the creek to reach a footbridge.

❷ Go over this and turn left then shortly afterwards turn right at a fingerpost marked Stackpole Quay. Walk above rocky outcrops, above the beach, to a gate. Follow the grassy path around the headland and back inland to a gate above Saddle Bay.

Continue around a large blowhole and up to a gate above a deeply cloven zawn (cleft), known as the Raming Hole.

3 Go through a gate a few hundred yards later and hug the coastline on your right to walk around Stackpole Head. As you turn back inland, pass a blowhole and then go through a gate to drop down to Barafundle Bay. Cross the back of the beach and climb up the steps on the other side to an archway in the wall. Continue through a gate and down some steps to Stackpole Quay.

4 Turn left, above the tiny harbour, and drop to pass the Old Boathouse Tearoom on your left before turning sharp right on to a road. Follow this past some buildings on the right and up to a T-junction, where you turn left.

5 Drop down into Stackpole village, pass the Stackpole Inn on the right, and continue around a series of bends until you come to a road on the left, over a bridge.

6 Cross the bridge and turn left to follow a good path along the side of the lake. Continue along this, ignoring a path off to the right, and turn left at a T-junction next to a building. Carry on along the lakeside to a bridge.

7 Don't cross the bridge, but drop down on to a narrow path that keeps straight ahead and follow it with the lake on your left. Continue ahead to another bridge, cross it, then carry on with the lake now on your right. This path leads to the footbridge that you crossed at Point **2**. Retrace your steps across the beach and up the steps back to the car park.

WHERE TO EAT AND DRINK St Govan's Inn at Bosherston is a hidden gem, with great food and a selection of real ales. The walls are often decorated with photographs of climbers in seemingly impossible positions on local cliffs. Dogs are allowed in the stable bar at the back.

WHAT TO SEE The views east from Stackpole Head stretch from Caldey Island – a religious enclave just off the coast of Tenby – to the Gower Peninsula in the distance. Beyond, to the south, you may be able to make out the lofty landform of Lundy Island and even the outline of the North Devon coast.

WHILE YOU'RE THERE Providing the footpath is open, take a stroll to St Govan's Chapel, a humble but spiritually uplifting stone building tucked away in a deep cleft in the cliffs, west of St Govan's Head. St Govan is thought to have been an Irish contemporary of St David and the story suggests that he was hiding from pirates in the cleft when a crack miraculously opened up in the floor. He entered and the crack then closed behind him, only opening again when the danger had passed. The present chapel dates from the 13th century, but probably incorporates some much older stonework.

Manobier and Swanlake Bay

DISTANCE 3 miles (4.8km)		MINIMUM TIME 1hr 30min	

ASCENT/GRADIENT 390ft (119m) ▲▲▲   LEVEL OF DIFFICULTY ✦✦✦

PATHS Coast path, clear paths across farmland

LANDSCAPE Sandy coves and dramatic coastline

SUGGESTED MAP OS Explorer OL36 South Pembrokeshire

START/FINISH Grid reference: SS063976

DOG FRIENDLINESS Difficult stiles, poop scoop on beaches. Keep on lead and off grass near house on The Dak

PARKING Pay-and-display car park by beach below castle

PUBLIC TOILETS At start

This is a delightful short walk that runs along the heads of some magnificent cliffs and visits a wonderful and remote sandy cove. The outward leg isn't particularly inspirational, but the narrow lane provides convenient access to the highest ground and the section across farmland is open and breezy, with fine views over the coast. Once reached, the narrow belt of white sand that makes up Swanlake Bay provides ample reward for your efforts. Flanked on both sides by impressive sandstone crags and cut off from easy road access by the farmland that you've just traversed, it sees few visitors and provides a stunning setting for a picnic.

GERALD'S PLEASANT SPOT

Once lauded by its most famous son, Giraldus Cambrensis, alias Gerald of Wales, as the 'pleasantest spot in Wales', Manorbier is these days best described as an attractive but sleepy coastal village dominated by a mighty castle and set among some of South Pembrokeshire's prettiest and most unspoilt countryside. Giraldus was born Gerald de Barri, the grandson of Odo, the first Norman Lord of the Manor, in 1146. He is best known for his attempts to set up an independent Church for Wales (a movement denied by Henry II) and for his chronicles of everyday life.

CALDEY ISLAND

The village name derives from 'Maenor of Pyrrus' or 'Manor of Pyr'. Pyrrus was the first Celtic abbot of Caldey, a nearby island first inhabited by monks in the 6th century AD and known in Welsh as Ynys Pyr, or Pyr's Island. Its landscape is wild and unspoilt and its buildings are inspirationally simple. There is a working Benedictine monastery and a number of ornate churches, including 12th-century St Illtyd's (sometimes known as St Illtud's), with its ancient sandstone cross.

MANORBIER CASTLE

Despite the profusion of well-preserved castles in this corner of Pembrokeshire, it still comes as a surprise to discover such an impressive edifice as Manorbier Castle tucked away in this tiny village. The original castle stems from the late 11th century, but the stone building that stands tall and proud over the beach and village these days was constructed in the early 12th century.

Since the de Barris, the castle has passed through many hands, including the Crown. It's now privately owned, but open to the public for tours. As well as the splendid views over the bay from the castle walls, you'll see many stately rooms, occupied these days by waxwork models of characters including Gerald, hard at work on his accounts.

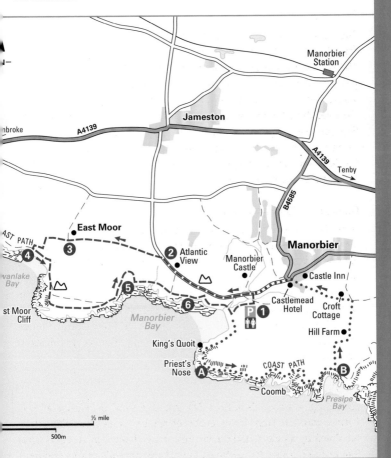

❶ Walk out of the car park entrance and turn left towards the sea. Stay on the road as it bears around to the right and climbs steeply above the coast. Pass the impressively situated and well-named Atlantic View cottage on your right before reaching a double gate on your left.

❷ Go through the gate and walk along the field-edge, with a bank and fence on your right, to reach a gate. Go through this and continue heading in the same direction to a gate close to the farm which you also pass through. Continue to a kissing gate by the farmhouse, which brings you into a small enclosure, then to another kissing gate that leads you away from the buildings.

❸ Continue again along the edge of the field to another kissing gate. Go through and turn left to drop down the field edge to a zig-zag that leads on to the coast path. Access to the beach is more or less directly beneath you.

❹ Turn left on to the coast path and go through a gate and steeply uphill. You'll eventually reach the top on a lovely airy ridge that swings east and then north to drop steeply down into a narrow dip above Manorbier Bay.

❺ Climb out of the dip to a gate and continue walking easily above the rocky beach. This path leads to a drive, beneath a large house.

❻ Continue beneath The Dak and uphill slightly to a gate, where the coast path drops off to the right. Follow this as it skirts a small car park and then winds down through the gorse and bracken to the beach. Cross the stream and turn left to follow a sandy track back to the car park.

WHERE TO EAT AND DRINK The Castle Inn, in the centre of Manorbier, is a cosy and friendly place with a good selection of food and a decent choice of ales. It boasts a great garden where you can sit and relax after a hard morning or afternoon's walk.

WHAT TO SEE The cliffs along this part of the coast show some dramatic irregularities in the old red sandstone that forms them. East Moor Cliff, the eastern headland of Swanlake Bay, is a prime example, with huge blocks creating impressive bastions. There are a few low-grade rock climbs on the cliff, which is huge and split by a very deep fissure.

WHILE YOU'RE THERE Tenby is the unofficial tourism capital of South Pembrokeshire and although its crowded streets and rows of hotels and B&Bs come as something of a shock after the more organic spots along the coast, it's still a charming, mainly Georgian, town with a beautiful harbour and plenty of attractions to keep you busy on a rainy day. Of particular historical interest are the original town walls. They were so effective that the Norman castle was made pretty much redundant.

Coastline and Cove

DISTANCE 5.5 miles (8.8km)   MINIMUM TIME 2hrs 30min

ASCENT/GRADIENT 580ft (177m) ▲▲▲   LEVEL OF DIFFICULTY ✛✛✛

SEE MAP AND INFORMATION PANEL FOR WALK 13

Leave Walk 13 after crossing the stream beyond Point **6** and cross the back of the beach to a set of steps that lead up to the coast path. Climb up through the bracken on a narrow path that shortly passes the impressive King's Quoit, a Stone Age burial chamber boasting a 16ft (4.8m) capstone supported by two smaller stones.

With fine views over Manorbier Beach and the sandstone headland crossed by Walk 13, continue up to the apex of the Priest's Nose, another sandstone headland with a number of caves (Point **A**). The path now passes close to a series of deeply cloven zawns, then turns east again to carve a narrow walkway across the steep hillside. The cliffs are lined by many steep slabs and bulky blocks that take the full force of any swell running.

At Coomb the trail turns inland again to round a steep-sided valley. Climb away from this and continue back out on to the headland; again the cliffs are propped up by magnificent rock formations. Next comes Presipe Bay, a narrow strip of secluded, bleached sand that appears almost smothered beneath such impressive cliffs (Point **B**). There's a wonderful viewpoint to the right of the path before it starts to descend. Access to the beach is via a set of steep steps in its western corner, but beware – the sands are pretty much covered at high tide so it's worth checking the timetable if you're hoping to spend time here.

At a gate bearing a notice about the nearby air defence range turn left, away from the coast, to walk up the edge of the field. Continue through a gate to a tree where a waymarker points you right to another gate. Go through. Go through this and follow the grassy track around Hill Farm to a point where it swings hard left. Go over a stile on the right and walk directly across the field to a waymarker by a telegraph pole. Continue through a gap in the wall, across another field to another stile. Keep straight ahead to a gap in a large wall and turn sharp left to cross a stile on to a surfaced drive. Pass Croft Cottage on your right and continue to a T-junction where you bear right. Follow this to the road, by the Castlemead Hotel. Turn left to walk down the road, back to the car park at the start of Walk 13.

Around Dinas Head

DISTANCE 3 miles (4.8km)	MINIMUM TIME 2hrs

ASCENT/GRADIENT 460ft (140m) ▲▲▲   LEVEL OF DIFFICULTY +++

PATHS Rough coastal path and a short section of easy, wheelchair-friendly track

LANDSCAPE Rugged cliffs with views over two sweeping bays

SUGGESTED MAP OS Explorer OL35 North Pembrokeshire

START/FINISH Grid reference: SN004399

DOG FRIENDLINESS Care on cliff tops and around livestock

PARKING Both sides of road by The Old Sailors, Pwllgwaelod Beach

PUBLIC TOILETS At start and Cwm-yr-Eglwys

Dinas Island, or Dinas Head as it's often known (Dinas Head is actually the headland at the island's northern apex), isn't actually an island at all. It's a rugged, sloping peninsula that's separated from the mainland by a shallow neck of flat marshy ground known as Cwm Dewi (David's Valley). This was formed at the end of the last ice age when a glacier blocked the outlet of Newport Bay, forcing watercourses westwards, beneath the ice. The shales and sandstones of the headland were eroded into a narrow channel. Island or not, this is a wonderful place to walk, encapsulating everything that's great about walking along a coast path.

The ruins of the tiny chapel of St Brynach dominate a pleasant green above the beach. Sheltered from the prevailing winds southwesterlies that pound this stretch of coast, Cwm-yr-Eglwys (Valley of the Church) often has the feel of a quaint Mediterranean hamlet, but on the night of 25 October 1859 it was subjected to one of the fiercest storms on record and the church was very battered. However, this was only a small part of the damage wreaked. That same fearful night, 114 ships were wrecked off the Welsh coast, with the loss of many lives. Another storm in 1979 all but completed the job of destruction – all that is left of the church today are the west wall and the tiny belfry.

The saint to whom the chapel was dedicated probably came from Ireland, where he would have been known as Bernach. According to the account of his life, written in the 12th century, he lived in the 6th century and visited both Rome and Brittany before arriving at what is now Milford Haven. He set about establishing various oratories in the area as well as a monastery at Nanhyfer, where he later died . Along the way, he had many adventures. In Llanfyrnach he turned down the advances of a young woman who retaliated by sending a horde of ruffians after him to kill him. Brynach survived and went on to drive out evil spirits; have a visitation from an angel (conveniently advising him to move on from a place where the locals had received him with some hostility); and perform various miracles, thus ensuring his posthumous rise to sainthood.

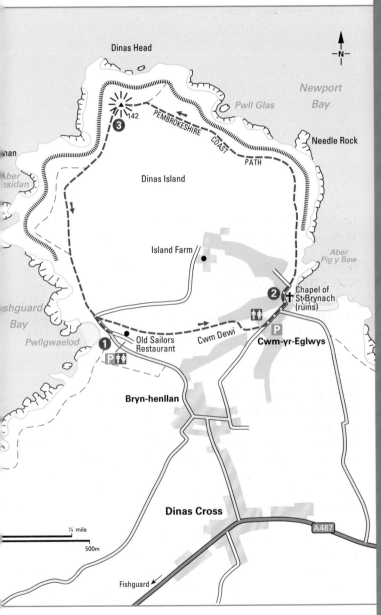

1 From the car park, make your way to the beach and bear right and then immediately right again, through a gate, to gain a well-surfaced path that follows the floor of Cwm Dewi. This wheelchair-friendly track is very popular so you'll probably meet other walkers as you pass the marshy ground to the right, which is a haven for butterflies. The path leads to a gate that in turn leads you through a caravan site and into the Cwm-yr-Eglwys car park. Turn left in the car park and follow a narrow path, which heads out towards the beach. The ruins of the tiny Chapel of St Brynach dominate a pleasant green above the beach.

2 Keep the ruins to your right and wander along the lane to a coast path waymarker on the right. Follow this steeply up steps to Aber Pig-y-Baw. The path emerges from the bushes and continues to cut easily around the hillside before steepening as it approaches the obvious sea stack of Needle Rock. Ignore the footpath off to left before this. This is a fine nesting site for a variety of seabirds and it appears positively congested

in late spring and early summer. Steps lead up the hillside to a gate from here and then the path continues to climb for over half a mile (800m) to the trig point that marks the top of the headland. This is a wonderfully lofty viewpoint and it is possible to scramble down a little way to the north if you fancy a sheltered rest stop.

3 The path now leads down above the western cliffs. Stay on the outside of the perimeter fence as it swings south again. Follow the coast down and wind your way through the gorse to a fork where you bear right (ignoring the yellow arrow pointing to the left) to the spur of Pen Castell. This tracks back inland again and drops to a gate above Pwllgwaelod Beach. From here you reach the road and can walk easily back past the Old Sailors restaurant to the beach and the car park.

WHERE TO EAT AND DRINK The Old Sailors licensed restaurant, adjacent to the car park, has replaced a pub called the Sailor's Safety Inn, which once showed a light to guide shipping. It specialises in seafood but it's also a good spot for a cream tea if that's all you need. Away from here, there's the popular Ship Aground, a grand public house in nearby Dinas Cross.

WHAT TO SEE The black and white birds usually seen on the steeper inner cliff of Needle Rock are guillemots and razorbills. Both are members of the auk family and it is difficult to tell them apart from a distance. The guillemot is actually a beautiful dark-chocolate colour and has a slim pointed bill, while the razorbill is more black in colour and close inspection of the head reveals that the bill is razor shaped, with thin white lines. You'll probably also notice a number of herring gulls on the fringes of the mêlée. These raucous gulls scavenge relentlessly, feeding on the eggs and chicks of the smaller auks. They will even steal the food from the parent birds' mouths.

WHILE YOU'RE THERE If the spiritual side of West Wales grabs your attention, you may enjoy the Saints and Stones Trail, a waymarked driving tour of some of the finest churches and religious sites in the area, many dating back to pre-Christian times. As well as St David's Cathedral, other highlights include the bleeding yew in St Brynach's. Leaflets describing the trail, which makes a big loop between Fishguard and St David's, are available from all the local tourist offices.

A Walk Above Newport

DISTANCE 5.5 miles (8.8km) MINIMUM TIME 3hrs 30min

ASCENT/GRADIENT 1,080ft (329m) ▲▲▲ LEVEL OF DIFFICULTY ✦✦✦

PATHS Easy coastal footpaths, boggy farm tracks, rough paths over bracken and heather-covered hillsides

LANDSCAPE Attractive harbour, farmland and rock-capped moor

SUGGESTED MAP OS Explorer OL35 North Pembrokeshire

START/FINISH Grid reference: SN057392

DOG FRIENDLINESS Care on roads, poop scoop on coast path section

PARKING Free car park opposite information centre, Long Street

PUBLIC TOILETS At start and near Parrog

Carn Ingli peeps over the shoulder of the small coastal town of Newport and it therefore makes sense to explore both in one walk. The coastal section is easy to follow and thoroughly enjoyable as the path traces a varied line along the Nyfer Estuary, at one stage following the actual sea wall itself. The tracks that cross the common, on the other hand, are rough and, in late summer, when the bracken is fully-grown, difficult to follow in places. They're worth sticking with though, for the views from the jagged rocks of the peak are among the best in the National Park.

NEWPORT

Once a busy port immersed predominantly in the wool trade, Newport was the former capital of the Marcher Lordship of Cemmaes, the only one to escape the abolition imposed by Henry VIII in the 16th-century Acts of Union. William Fitz-Martin, who moved to Newport from nearby Nevern, granted a number of privileges to the town, including the election of its own mayor, something which it still has to this day, and the beating of the bounds on horseback by the mayor, which takes place every August. Its castle, once the home of the aforementioned lord, has since been incorporated into a mansion house and is now in private ownership.

THE ROCK OF ANGELS

Often described as one of the most sacred sites in Britain, the lofty heights of Carn Ingli were well known by the mystical St Brynach, who scaled them in order to commune with angels. After a life of persecution – the Irish-born saint was made most unwelcome by the Welsh when he returned from his pilgrimage to the Holy Land – he finally settled in Nevern, where he built his church. It remains one of the most visited in Pembrokeshire due to its ancient Celtic cross and a yew tree that appears to actually bleed. A second cross, carved into the rocky hillside, has seen so many visitors that the stones beneath it are now as smooth as glass. Judging from the remains of both Iron Age fortresses and Bronze Age huts, there was human activity on Mynydd Carningli long before Christianity. The size of the settlements suggests that the windswept hillside would have once supported fairly large communities. Perhaps the existence of standing stones near by demonstrates that these early settlers were also aware of the mountain's special powers.

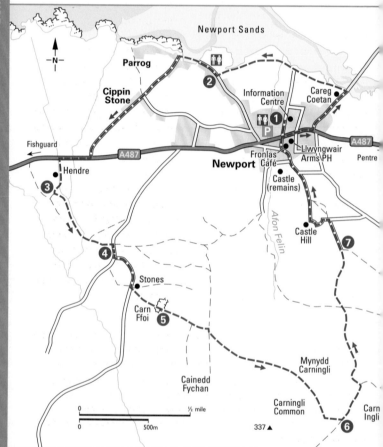

● Turn right out of the car park in Long Street and left on to East Street. Fork left into Pen y Bont and continue to the bridge, where a waymarked footpath leads off to the left. Follow this along the banks of the estuary to a small road.

● Turn right on the road and walk past the toilets to its end, where the path then follows the sea wall. Continue to another lane and turn left to follow it up to the A487. Turn right on to this road, then turn left to continue walking up the drive of Hendre farm.

❸ Pass the farmhouse on your right to go through the gate and follow the track to another gate where you turn left to follow a small stream. The path emerges on to open ground and hugs the left edge of the field to reach another gate. Continue in the same line along a hedged section, which is boggy for most of the year. Climb over a stile and keep straight ahead to climb up to the road.

❹ Turn right on to the road and then fork left to continue past some houses to a pair of huge upright stones on the left. Pass through these stones and follow the faint track up to a rocky tor. Head up from this towards the larger tor of Carn Ffoi. From the top of here you'll be able to pick up a clearer path that leads through an old field system defined by small, ruined walls. Navigate your way through the old fields heading southeast to the right-hand side of a fenced field.

❺ Now bear half-right on to a clear footpath (to the left of the path that runs between lines of low gorse) that leads across the hillside, aiming towards the obvious top of Carn Ingli, which will come into view as you climb. Fork left after 50yds (46m) and then continue across the hillside beneath the high point of Carningli Common. The path bears right to climb into the saddle between Carningli Common and the rocky top of Mynydd Carningli. Continue to the far end of the rocky ridge and then bear left to follow a faint path up on to the ridge top.

❻ Carry on to Carn Ingli and bear left along the path to pass in front of it, to join a good, clear track that runs straight down the hillside. Continue on this, keeping straight ahead at two crossroads. This drops you down to a gate in a corner, where a path leads on to a concrete track.

❼ Take the lane to a T-junction and turn left. Follow this road down to a junction in College Square, where you turn left. This is Church Street. Continue into the centre and turn right into Market Street to reach the main road, which you cross into Long Street.

WHERE TO EAT AND DRINK The Llwyngwair Arms is one of the best pubs in this part of Pembrokeshire, with good beer and a local but friendly atmosphere. The Fronlas Café in Market Street is a great place for a snack or a cuppa.

WHAT TO SEE On your left, as you approach the bridge along Pen-y-Bont, you'll find the rather understated Careg Coetan, an impressive cromlech or burial chamber tucked away behind holiday bungalows. In common with many such sites in Wales, it's said to be the final resting place of the legendary King Arthur.

WHILE YOU'RE THERE Small lanes lead east from Newport to Pentre Ifan, one of the finest megalithic cromlechs in the British Isles. Over 4,000 years old, the giant 16ft (4.8m) capstone sits on a selection of smaller supports that hold it some 6ft (1.8m) above ground. It is thought that the builders of these magnificent tombs believed by constructing them on high ground the interred souls of the dead would be placed closer to the spirits and the bringer of life, the sun. It would have originally been covered with a mound of earth, but this has since eroded away.

In the Preseli Hills

DISTANCE 5.5 miles (8.8km)	MINIMUM TIME 2hrs 30min

ASCENT/GRADIENT 560ft (171m) ▲▲▲   LEVEL OF DIFFICULTY ✦✦✦

PATHS Mainly clear paths across open moorland

LANDSCAPE Rolling hills topped with rocky outcrops

SUGGESTED MAP AA Walker's Map 17 Brecon & The Black Mountains

START/FINISH Grid reference: SN165331

DOG FRIENDLINESS Care needed near livestock

PARKING Small lay-by on lane beneath Foel Drygarn

PUBLIC TOILETS None on route

NOTES Navigation very difficult in poor visibility

A circular walk around the most interesting sites of the Preseli Hills is almost impossible. The uplands form an isolated east-west ridge that would at best form one side of a circuit linked with a lengthy road section. Instead of taking this less-than-ideal option, this walk forms a contorted and narrow figure-of-eight that scales the most spectacular hill on the ridge, traces the line of the famous dolerite outcrops, or carns, and then makes an out-and-back sortie to an impressive stone circle. Convoluted it may be, but it's packed with interest and easy going enough for most people to complete comfortably.

PRESELI HILLS

The Pembrokeshire Coast National Park is best known for its stunning coastline. Britain's smallest National Park is in no single place further than 10 miles (16.1km) from the sea. This furthest point was a deliberate extension of the boundaries to incorporate one of the most important historic sites in the United Kingdom, the Preseli Hills.

CARN MENYN'S BLUESTONES

It was from Carn Menyn, one of the rocky tors that crown the marshy and often windswept hills, that the bluestones forming the inner circle of Stonehenge were taken. These bluestones, or spotted dolerite stones to give them their proper name, would have each weighed somewhere in the region of 4 tonnes and must have been transported over 200 miles (320km) in total. To this day we cannot explain how or why.

ANCIENT ROAD

The Stonehenge story, significant as it may be, is only part of the historic and, at times, mystical feel of this narrow, grassy upland. The track that follows the ridge is an ancient road, perhaps dating back over 5,000 years. It's probable that it was a safe passage between the coast and the settlements inland at a time when wild predators such as bears and wolves roamed the valleys below. Standing stones dot the hillsides and gravestones line the track, most likely those of travellers or traders who were buried where they died.

BEDDARTHUR

West of Carn Menyn, beneath another impressive outcrop named Carn Bica, there's a stone circle known as Beddarthur. Small by comparison to Stonehenge or Avebury, its oval arrangement of stones, each measuring 2ft-3ft (0.6m-1m) is said to be yet another burial place of King Arthur; 'bedd' means grave in Welsh. There are certainly links between the legendary historical superhero and the area; it's suggested that the King and his knights chased Twrch Trywyth, the magical giant boar, across these hills before heading east.

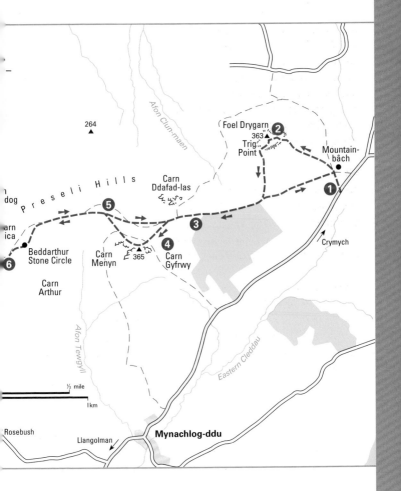

1 From the lay-by on the lane from Crymych, walk straight up a stony track opposite, then turn right up a stony track. When you reach three gates, keep going straight ahead for another 100yds (91m) or so, and then fork left on to a grassy track, which soon becomes clearer as it winds its way up the hillside. Follow this all the way to the rocky cairns and trig point on Foel Drygarn.

2 Bear left at the summit and locate a grassy track that drops steeply to the south. Cross the heather-clad plateau beneath, aiming for the left-hand corner of a wood. When you meet the main track, turn right to walk with the edge of the wood on your left.

3 Leaving the wood, the path climbs slightly to some rocky tors. As you pass the tor to the left of the track, the path forks and you follow the left-hand track to the nearest of the group of outcrops to your left.

4 This is Carn Gyfrwy. Continue on faint paths to the larger outcrops ahead, then curve right away from the stones and drop slightly to Carn Menyn, the lowest of the bunch, perched precariously on the edge of the escarpment. The path becomes clearer here and drops slightly into a marshy saddle that can be seen ahead.

5 In the saddle you'll meet the main track. Turn left and follow it steadily up towards Carn Bica, which is visible on the hillside ahead of you. Just before this, you'll cross the circle made by the stones of Beddarthur.

6 Turn around and retrace your steps back to the saddle. Climb slightly to pass the tor where you turned left to Carn Gyfrwy on your way out, ignoring the paths forking right to Carn Menyn, and stay on this main path to walk beside the plantation once more, now on your right. At the end of this, continue straight on, following a fence-topped wall to your right, down to the gate. Turn right on to the lane and continue back to the car park.

WHERE TO EAT AND DRINK There's nothing on the route so it's best to head west to Rosebush where the Tafarn Sinc does good food and welcomes children in the eating area before 9pm. There's also decent food to be found at the New Inn (Tafarn Newydd), located on the main road on the other side of the village.

WHILE YOU'RE THERE Slate quarrying was once big business in the Preseli Hills and the remnants of this activity are still visible in places like Rosebush, to the west. If you'd like to see the kind of thing that can be crafted out of the smooth, flat stones, take a look at the Slate Workshop at Llangolman, where authentic Welsh slate is still put to good effect in a variety of craft items.

Right: The Preseli Hills near Rosebush (Walk 17)

The Highs and Lows of Rhossili Bay

DISTANCE 4 miles (6.4km) MINIMUM TIME 1hr 45min

ASCENT/GRADIENT 590ft (180m) ▲▲▲ LEVEL OF DIFFICULTY ✦✦✦

PATHS Easy-to-follow footpaths across grassy downs

LANDSCAPE Rolling downland, rocky outcrops and views over a gorgeous sandy beach

SUGGESTED MAP OS Explorer 164 Gower

START/FINISH Grid reference: SS416880

DOG FRIENDLINESS Care needed near livestock

PARKING Large car park at end of road in Rhossili

PUBLIC TOILETS At start

The Gower Peninsula comprises a 15-mile (24km) finger of land pointing westwards from the urban sprawl of Swansea. Its southern coast is spectacular, with dune-backed beaches of surf-swept, clean yellow sand and magnificent limestone cliffs, chiselled in places into deep gullies and knife-edge ridges. The northern coast forms the southern fringes of the marshy Loughor Estuary and is an important habitat for wading birds and other marine life. Between the two coastlines, the land rises into a series of whaleback ridges covered with gorse, heather and bracken and littered with prehistoric remains. Scattered around the landscape are a number of castles. In 1957, the peninsula was designated Britain's first Area of Outstanding Natural Beauty (AONB).

RHOSSILI BAY AND DOWN

Of all the Gower beaches, none are blessed with quite the untamed splendour of Rhossili Bay. It's sweeping expanse of golden sand runs for over 4 miles (6.4km) from the headland of the Worms Head to the stranded outcrop of Burry Holms, upon which sits a ruined monastic chapel. It owes much of its wild nature to the steep-sided down that provides a natural and impenetrable barrier to development. The down is a 633ft (193m) high, whaleback ridge that runs almost the full length of the beach. The path that traces the ridge is one the fairest places to walk in the whole of South Wales, especially in late summer when the heather tinges the hillsides pink. From The Beacon, at the southern end of the ridge, it's often possible to see St Govan's Head in Pembrokeshire and even the North Devon coastline on a very clear day.

The string of tiny islets at the bay's southernmost tip is known as the Worms Head. Now a nature reserve, it is reached at low tide by scrambling across the rocky causeway at the tip of the promontory.

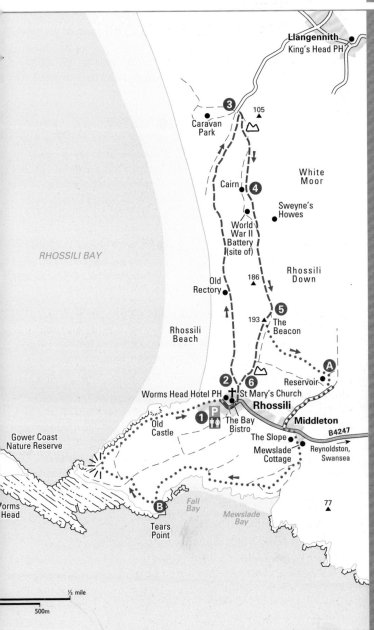

① From the car park, head out on to the road and continue uphill as if you were walking back out of the village. You'll pass St Mary's Church on your left then, immediately after this, bear left down on a broad track to a gate at its end. Go through this and keep

left to follow a grassy track that snakes along the steep hillside.

② Follow this through the bracken, passing the Old Rectory on your left and eventually you'll reach a sunken section with a wall on your left, and a caravan park behind. Don't be tempted to break off right just yet; instead, keep going until you come to a gate by a road on the left.

3 Don't go through but turn sharp right and follow the grassy track steeply up on to the ridge. At the top of the steep section where the path isn't always clear it's easy to be drawn off to the right towards some obvious outcrops, but keep to the top track that literally follows the crest.

4 You'll pass some ancient cairns and drop slightly to pass a pair of megalithic cromlechs, or burial chambers. These are known as

Sweyne's Howes and are over 4,000 years old. More obviously, you'll spot the remains of a World War II anti-aircraft battery to the right. Continue on a broad track up to the high point of The Beacon.

5 Keep straight ahead on a clear track that starts to drop easily then steepens to meet a dry-stone wall. Continue walking down the side of the wall and you'll eventually come to the gate you passed through on the way out.

6 Follow the lane out to the road, turn right and pass St Mary's Church on your right to return to the car park.

WHERE TO EAT AND DRINK One option is to walk 0.5 miles (800m) from Point **3** to Llangennith village, where the excellent, dog-friendly King's Head serves great food and real ale. Otherwise, there are a few places to get a cuppa and a snack in Rhossili; from the Bay View Shop, which offers hot snacks and has a few tables outside, to the excellent The Bay Bistro & Coffee House, which serves breakfast and lunches during the day and top-notch restaurant food in the evenings. The Worms Head Hotel is the only pub in the village, but if you don't mind driving a few miles, the King Arthur Hotel at Reynoldston has a better atmosphere and serves better food. None of the Rhossili options are dog friendly.

WHAT TO SEE More than one ship has fallen foul of the cruel storms that pound Rhossili and the wreckage of a few of these still pepper the beach. The most obvious is the *Helvetica*, now a crumbled timber skeleton protruding from the sands at low tide. She was washed up here in November 1887, but miraculously her five-man crew all survived.

WHILE YOU'RE THERE About 0.5 miles (800m) east of Reynoldston there's a footpath that leads to King Arthur's Stone, one of the finest standing cromlechs (burial chambers) in Wales, covered with an enormous capstone. The site is believed to be over 6,000 years old and is most striking when visited at sunrise or sunset.

Right: Rhossili Bay at sunset (Walk 18)

Rhossili and Mewslade Bay

DISTANCE 7 miles (11.3km)   MINIMUM TIME 3hrs

ASCENT/GRADIENT 650ft (198m) ▲▲▲   LEVEL OF DIFFICULTY ✦✦✦

SEE MAP AND INFORMATION PANEL FOR WALK 18

While Walk 18 reveals the magnificent sweep of Rhossili Bay, what it doesn't show are the rugged limestone bluffs and headlands that make up the bulk of the peninsula's southern coast. For that reason, providing you've got both the energy and the time, it's well worth descending to the left of the trig point and dropping down to the rocky gash that forms the secluded Mewslade Bay (a trip to the beach is optional). Returning to Rhossili from here, you get a taster of the rugged rock-strewn landscape that's explored in more detail in Walk 20 and you also get a bird's-eye view over the Gower's most distinctive landmark, the rocky islets of the Worms Head.

From the trig point on The Beacon (Point ❺), keep ahead for about 50yds (45m) and then fork left and go straight over at a crossroads to follow the track easily along a blunt spur. This descends to a small covered reservoir and the head of a gravel track. Follow this beneath the reservoir (Point ❹) and down to a lane, where you turn right. Follow the lane down to the B4247 and cross the road. Turn left on to the pavement and follow this along until, between two dwellings called The Slope and Mewslade Cottage, you turn right by a sign to Mewslade on to a hedged lane. Follow this down to a gate. Continue straight ahead if you fancy getting your toes wet; if you don't, turn right on to the bracken-covered heathland.

The path drops into a shallow dip and then forks. Take the left-hand track, which heads uphill through the bracken on to an open headland above Mewslade Bay. Follow the coast around to the right and pass through some spectacular limestone outcrops and above some impressive cliffs before being funnelled into a narrow section by a wall. The path is obvious from this point as it crosses above Fall Bay and then climbs up towards Tears Point, Point ❷. Continue to hug the wall until it dips into a valley, then bear slightly left to follow the cliffs around to the western end of the headland.

If the tides are right, it's possible to drop down from here to cross on to the Worms Head. If not, bear right and follow the path along the cliff line until it meets the wall again. From here, continue easily back towards Rhossili on a well-surfaced track that leads to the road and on to the car park at Point ❶.

Port Eynon to Rhossili

DISTANCE 6.5 miles (10.4km)   MINIMUM TIME 3hrs

ASCENT/GRADIENT 850ft (259m) ▲▲▲   LEVEL OF DIFFICULTY +++

PATHS Coast paths

LANDSCAPE Limestone cliffs and sheltered bays

SUGGESTED MAP OS Explorer 164 Gower

START Grid reference: SS467851   FINISH Grid reference: SS416881

DOG FRIENDLINESS Generally fine on bus, care around livestock and on steep cliffs. Generally fine on bus

PARKING Large car park in Port Eynon

PUBLIC TOILETS At start and at Rhossili

The stretch of coast from Port Eynon along to Rhossili marks the far southwestern extent of the Gower peninsula and includes one of the most iconic sights in Wales: Worms Head. The sandy beach of Port Eynon Bay, though far from large, somehow manages to encompass two villages – Horton and Port Eynon, from where this walk sets off. While less undulating than some of the coastal paths around South Wales, there are still enough dips and climbs in the middle section of this route to get the heart pumping as you pass a brace of Iron Age forts and Paviland Cave. Journey's end is at Rhossili, a tiny village popular with day-trippers, where refreshment awaits, along with a bus to take you back to Port Eynon.

In Victorian times, Port Eynon was a bustling place whose men worked in local quarries, fished for oysters or served as mariners. The place is a lot quieter now – the sandy beach providing the main attraction. The 12th-century church of St Cattwg is worth a look before you set off. Though 'renovated' by the Victorians in their habitually intrusive manner, they didn't touch the Norman doorway and in the porch you can still see the stoup (for holding holy water), which is reputed to have been donated by a Spanish sea captain saved from drowning by local people.

WORMS HEAD

A mile-long island spearing the Bristol Channel, Worms Head can be reached at low tide by crossing a rocky natural causeway. On the Inner Head there once stood an ancient promontory fort, at which spot a young Dylan Thomas fell asleep, missed the tide and had to wait from dusk until midnight until the next one, fortified only by a bag of sandwiches and a book. He later recalled being terrified by the experience, although he immortalised it in his short story *Who Do You Wish Was With Us?*

1 At low tide, walk on to the beach following coast path waymarkers to the Salthouse ruins. If the tide's high, follow a good track past the car park and through a gate to the Youth Hostel, which you keep to your left to continue on a caravan park drive to the ruins down on your left. From here, follow the sandy track along the coast until, in the centre of the rocky bay to your left, the path splits. Take the right-hand fork and climb steeply taking the left fork when the path splits again past a quarry on your right to the monument on the hilltop.

2 Follow the cliff tops until the path drops down to a gate. Cross this and walk behind the rocky beach. Ignore the path off to the right half-way across the beach and when the path forks, keep left to another gate marked Overton Cliffs. Keep ahead to follow the path as it squeezes between impressive limestone cliffs and steep scree. The path sneaks through rocky outcrops then heads down to a wall. Go through the gate, turn right and follow the path steeply upwards to meet a good path.

3 Turn left on to this and follow the wall. This section continues to follow the coast path, until you reach the deeply cloven gorge of Foxhole Slade.

4 Keep ahead in the dip through a gate and climb steeply back up. To your left, but almost impossible to reach, is Paviland Cave. Continue along the wall and through another gate. After 100yds (91m), next to a wooden gate on the right, fork left and continue until you join the wall again and drop to a gate. Cross this and bear left to head back out on to the cliff top.

5 Here you'll find the earthworks of an Iron Age fort. A wall splits the ramparts; cross this through a gate and follow the coast around to a fence, which you then follow to the head of a huge hollow with no name on the OS map. Go behind this bearing slightly right at the crossroads of paths by a stile (which you don't cross) and continue along the line of the wall, which initially hugs the coast before heading back inland a little as it approaches Mew Slade. As the wall turns sharp right, keep straight ahead to a steep path that drops down awkwardly into Mew Slade.

6 From the bottom of the dip, vertigo sufferers should continue along the coast path to avoid an extremely narrow path above a precipitous drop. Everyone else should turn left after the gate to follow a grassy path coastwards to the small cove, hidden behind rocky outcrops and covered almost completely by the sea at high tide. A narrow path heads west from the beach and contours around the steep hillside to rejoin the main coast path in an area of outstanding limestone scenery. Bear left on to the path here and follow it around to another dip. Keep high to round the head of the valley and then drop down, towards Tears Point. Head back up the grassy down towards the cliff tops, where you veer around to the right to follow them along. The main path actually hugs the wall all the way back to Rhossili, but a more enjoyable option is to continue around the coast passing above the Worms Head and then swinging north at Kitchen Corner to rejoin the main, well-surfaced track as you approach Rhossili village. Continue past the visitor centre and the main car park to the bus stop, on the left just before the church. There are five buses a day in each direction weekdays and a circular shuttle service at weekends (in season).

Woodland at Oxwich Point

DISTANCE 4.5 miles (7.2km)   MINIMUM TIME 2hrs

ASCENT/GRADIENT 480ft (146m) ▲▲▲   LEVEL OF DIFFICULTY ✚✚✚

PATHS Clear paths through woodland, along coast and across farmland, quiet ane

LANDSCAPE Mixed woodland and rugged coastline

SUGGESTED MAP OS Explorer 164 Gower

START/FINISH Grid reference: SS500864

DOG FRIENDLINESS Can mostly run free but watch steep cliffs and livestock

PARKING Oxwich Bay

PUBLIC TOILETS Opposite Oxwich Bay Hotel near start

The Gower has less obvious headlands than nearby Pembrokeshire and this makes it much more difficult to fashion short but interesting circular walks. This one stands out for a couple of reasons. Firstly, it can be combined with a visit to Oxwich National Nature Reserve, a treasure trove of marshland and sand dunes in a wonderful beachside location. Secondly, the wonderful coastal scenery includes the beautiful and usually deserted beach known as The Sands. And finally, being short, it allows plenty of time for exploring both the atmospheric St Illtyd's Church and the majestic ruins of Oxwich Castle.

OXWICH VILLAGE

Once a busy port that paid its way by shipping limestone from quarries on the rugged headland, Oxwich is now one of the prettiest and most unspoilt Gower villages, due in no small part to its distance from the main roads. The name is derived from Axwick, Norse for Water Creek. For maximum enjoyment, it's best visited away from the crowd-filled main holiday seasons.

ST ILLTYD'S

Founded in the 6th century AD and tucked away in a leafy clearing above the beach, St Illtyd's Church is particularly significant for its stone font, which is said to have been donated by St Illtyd himself. The grounds are tranquil with an atmosphere that comes in stark contrast to the summertime chaos of the beach below. Behind the building is the grave of an unknown soldier who was washed up on the beach during World War II. It's certainly a spooky spot and the graveyard is purported to be haunted by a strange half-man-half-horse creature. St Illtyd (or St Illtud) was a Welsh-born monk who founded the nearby abbey of Llanilltud Fawr (Llantwit Major). He is perhaps most famous for his fights against famine which included sailing grain ships to Brittany. He died in Brittany in AD 505.

FEUDING FAMILIES

Really a 16th-century mansion house built by Sir Rhys Mansel on the site of the 14th-century castle, Oxwich Castle occupies an airy setting above the bay. Sir Rhys, in common with many Gower locals, wasn't above plundering the cargo of ships that came to grief in the bay and was quick to take advantage of a French wreck in late December 1557. The salvage rights, however, belonged to a Sir George Herbert of Swansea, who quickly paid Mansel a visit to reclaim his goods. A fight broke out and Sir Rhys's daughter Anne was injured by a stone thrown by Herbert's servant. She later died from her injuries. Court action against Herbert proved ineffective and there followed a feud which continued for many years until eventually the Mansel family moved to Margam, east of Swansea. Part of the mansion was leased to local farmers, but most of the fine building fell into disrepair.

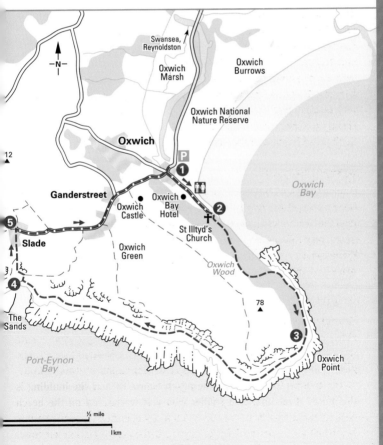

1 Walk out of the car park and turn left to a crossroads. Turn left here (waymarked 'Eglwys') and pass the Woodside Guesthouse and the Oxwich Bay Hotel, on your right. This lane leads into the woods and up to 6th-century St Illtyd's Church, where a gate marks the end of the road and the start of a path leading out on to Oxwich Point.

2 Join the path that runs beneath the church, and follow it for a few paces before going up wooden steps that climb steeply into the wood. Just before the top of the steps turn left to go through the wood, dropping back down a veritable glut of steps and around the headland until it comes out into the open above Oxwich Point.

3 The path drops through gorse and bracken to become a grassy coast path that runs easily above a rocky beach. Keep the sea on your left and ignore any tracks that run off to the right. After approximately 1 mile (1.6km) you'll pass a distinct valley that drops in from your right. Continue past this and you'll be funneled into a narrow, fenced section with a field to your right. Go through a couple of gates, and you'll eventually reach a path diversion that points you right, away from the beach.

4 Follow this to a kissing gate and a broad farm track, where you turn left. Continue up and around to the right until you come to a galvanised kissing gate. Go through this and keep right to head up a lane past some houses to a crossroads with a lane on your left marked Western Slade Farm.

5 Turn right here and follow the road along to a fork where you keep right. Pass through the hamlets of Oxwich Green and Ganderstreet. Drop down to the entrance of Oxwich Castle on the right. After looking at or exploring the castle, turn right, back on to the lane, and head down into Oxwich village. Keep straight ahead to the car park.

WHERE TO EAT AND DRINK Snacks are available in Oxwich - try the Beach Hut or the General Stores - and there's also the Oxwich Bay Hotel, which you pass on the walk, serving food all day from bar snacks to daily specials (children's meals also available). But, for the best food and atmosphere in this part of the Gower, it's worth heading to the King Arthur Hotel in Reynoldston.

WHAT TO SEE Spring is a great time to wander the woods of Oxwich Point where many interesting flowers can be seen vying for space before the deciduous canopy develops, cutting out the light supply. Perhaps the most prolific is ramsons, or wild garlic as it's also known. It isn't actually related to garlic, but when the woodland floor is completely carpeted by the stunning white flowers, the smell certainly resembles it.

WHILE YOU'RE THERE A windswept pot-pourri of dunes, saltwater marshes and freshwater pools, Oxwich National Nature Reserve offers an unusual and important habitat to many species of flora and fauna. Wild orchids are prolific in spring and early summer and the reserve is also an important breeding ground for a few species of butterfly, including the small blue, brown argus and marbled white. There are a number of trails that cross the marshes.

The Glamorgan Heritage Coast

DISTANCE 6 miles (9.7km)	MINIMUM TIME 2hrs 30min

ASCENT/GRADIENT 460ft (140m) ▲▲▲   LEVEL OF DIFFICULTY ✦✦✦

PATHS Easy-to-follow across farmland and coastline

LANDSCAPE Deciduous woodland, farmland, bracken-covered sand dunes and rocky coastline

SUGGESTED MAP OS Explorer 151 Cardiff & Bridgend

START/FINISH Grid reference: SS885731

DOG FRIENDLINESS Some difficult stiles; no dogs allowed on beach at Dunraven in summer

PARKING Large car park at Heritage Centre above Dunraven Beach

PUBLIC TOILETS Heritage Centre, also at Ogmore

Most visitors to South Wales overlook the land that lies south of the M4 between Cardiff and Swansea. Yet surprisingly, smack bang between the two cities and overshadowed by the huge industrial complexes of Port Talbot, there is an unspoilt strip of coast.

Granted Heritage Coast status in 1972, the 14-mile (22.5km) stretch of coastline that runs between Ogmore and Gileston stands as defiant against progress as its cliffs do against the huge ebbs and flows of the Bristol Channel tides. Sandy beaches, often punctuated by weathered strips of rock that dip their toes in the ocean, break up an otherwise formidable barrier of limestone and shale cliffs that rise and dip gracefully above the turbulent grey waters. It's fair to say that the scenery doesn't quite match the breathtaking beauty of the Gower Peninsula or Pembrokeshire, but somehow the unkempt wildness has an appeal all of its own.

HERITAGE CENTRE

Dunraven Bay houses the Heritage Centre, which offers displays and information about the area. It also makes an appropriate starting point for a walk that gives at least a taster of this unique landscape. The early stages track inland, through woodland and farmland before heading coastwards, at the small village of St Bride's Major. From here, the path sneaks between dunes and drops to the Ogmore River. Following the estuary downstream through bracken that simply teems with wildlife, you'll meet the coast at Ogmore-by-Sea and pick up the coast path above one of many beaches here. With ocean views to your right and the dunes to your left, you'll now climb easily back up above Dunraven.

The Glamorgan Heritage Coast was one of three pilot schemes set up in 1972 to protect the country's unique coastal landscapes and environments from destructive development. There are now 43 such areas in England and Wales, and in Wales they account for over 40 per cent of the total coastline. The aims of the scheme are fourfold; to maintain the ecological diversity, to provide public access and encourage recreational use, to protect the needs of the local population, including farmers and landowners, and to preserve the quality of the coastline. The Glamorgan Heritage Coast is managed by the Countryside Council for Wales which employs a professional ranger service to take care of the area.

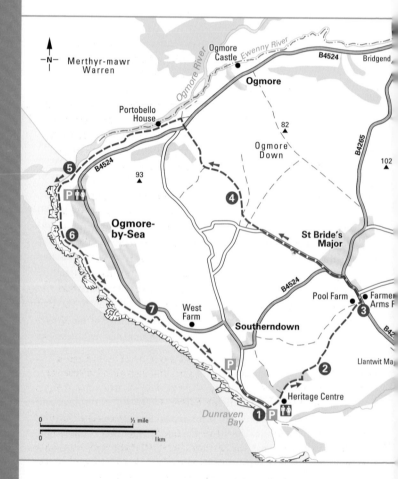

1 From the car park, head up the lane at the back of the car park and pass the Heritage Centre on the right. Keep walking straight ahead as the road swings left and go through a gate next to a stile to duck into woodland. Continue to a fork by a waymarker and a gap in the wall, where you keep left to reach a stile. Cross this stile and walk along the edge of the field to reach a stile on your left. Go over the stile, then cross a stone stile on your right to keep ahead with a hedge to your right.

2 Cross into another field and keep to the left-hand side, following the hedgerow, which is now on your left. When you reach the next stile, continue ahead, go past a gate on the left, to reach another stone stile on the left. Cross this stile and head right over another stile, next to a gate, to another stone stile between a house and the farmyard.

3 Turn left on to the road and walk into the village. Keep left into the Southerndown road then fork right into Heol-y-slough. Follow this road for 0.75 miles (1.2km) then, as the road bends left, continue across the common. Keep ahead where a bridleway crosses the track. As you join another track, maintain your direction along the valley floor.

4 The path winds its way down through sand dunes, passing a tributary valley on the left, and eventually emerges on the B4524. Cross the road and continue towards the river until you locate one of the many paths that lead left, parallel to

the river, towards Portobello House. Keep left on the drive then, once above the house, continue along a clear path, again parallel to the Ogmore River.

5 Make sure you stay above the small cliffs as you approach the mouth of the estuary and you'll eventually arrive at a huge car parking area above the beach. Go through the car park along the coast around to the left.

6 You'll come to a stone wall, which will funnel you through a gate marked 'Coast Path'. Continue along the coast path until, 0.75 miles (1.2km) from the gate, you meet with a very steep-sided valley. Turn left into this valley then turn immediately right, on to a footpath that climbs steeply up the grassy hillside.

7 Stay with the footpath as it follows the line of a dry-stone wall around to West Farm. Keep the wall to the left to continue to the upper car park. A gap in the wall, at the side of this, leads you to a grassy track that follows the road down into Dunraven.

WHERE TO EAT AND DRINK Along the route you'll pass the Farmers Arms in St Bride's Major. This is a family-orientated pub that does good bar food and also has a separate restaurant (no dogs allowed). Another option is a short detour into Ogmore-by-Sea where there's plenty of choice.

WHAT TO SEE If the sea seems a long way out, it's worth remembering that the tidal flows in the Bristol Channel are the second largest in the world, with the differences between high and low water being well over 39ft (12m) on a high spring tide. The only larger tides are witnessed in Canada's Bay of Fundy.

WHILE YOU'RE THERE Only a mile (1.6km) from Ogmore-by-Sea is Ogmore Castle, a 12th-century Norman fortification that lies in a pretty green valley and is reputed to be the place where King Arthur was fatally wounded. His body is said to be buried in a cave near by. True or not, the ruins are very basic but incredibly atmospheric.

Along the Waterfalls

DISTANCE 4 miles (6.4km)   MINIMUM TIME 2hrs

ASCENT/GRADIENT 360ft (110m) ▲▲▲   LEVEL OF DIFFICULTY ✦✦✦

PATHS Riverside paths and forest tracks, some rough sections and steps

LANDSCAPE Wooded valleys, fast flowing rivers, waterfalls

SUGGESTED MAP AA Walker's Map 18 West & Central Brecon Beacons

START/FINISH Grid reference: SN928124

DOG FRIENDLINESS Rivers too powerful for fetching sticks and care needed near steep drops

PARKING Park car park at Porth yr Ogof, near Ystradfellte

PUBLIC TOILETS At start

In a National Park justly renowned for its sweeping, but barren, mountain scenery, lovers of high ground are in danger of completely overlooking one the Brecon Beacons' hidden gems. This is the pocket of dramatic limestone scenery often referred to as Waterfall Country. South of the upland plateaux of Fforest Fawr, geological faults and water erosion have produced a series of deep, narrow gorges, sheltered by impressive woodland and randomly broken up by a succession of gushing waterfalls. The highlight of this is Sgwd yr Eira, where it's possible to venture right behind the falls. Walking here is a completely different experience to that of the windswept escarpments, but the scenery is marvellous and the generally sheltered nature of the terrain makes it an ideal outing for those days when cloud obscures the peaks.

HARD SANDSTONE SHELVES

In simple terms, the falls are the result of a geological fault that pushed the hard sandstone, which makes up the backbone of most of the National Park, up against softer shales. The force of the rivers, which spring up high on the mountains of Fforest Fawr, has eroded the shales leaving shelves of the harder rock exposed. These shelves are clearly visible on most of the waterfalls.

CAVES AND SINKHOLES

At the southern edge of the high ground, a layer of carboniferous limestone overlies the old red sandstone. This younger rock is soluble in the slightly acidic rain and river water that constantly pounds it. The erosion results in caves like Porth yr Ogof at the start of this walk, where the rivers literally disappear underground, and craters where rainwater exploits weaknesses and faults in the rock – these are often referred to as sinkholes or shake holes.

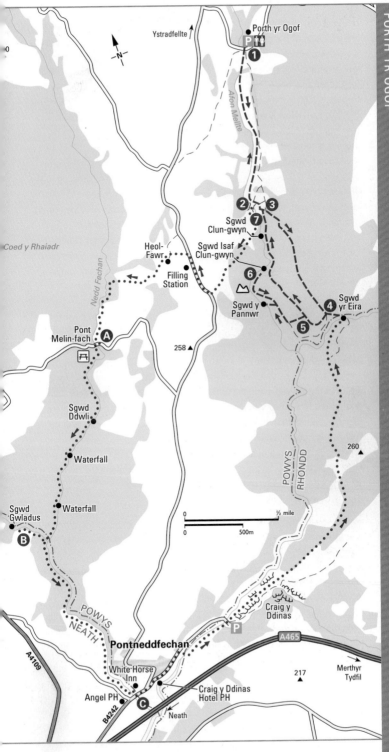

Ystradfellte ↑

Porth yr Ogof

P ♨ ①

Afon Mellte

N

② ③

Sgwd ⑦
Clun-gwyn

Sgwd Isaf
Clun-gwyn

Heol-
Fawr

Filling
Station

Coed y Rhaiadr

⑥

Sgwd y
Pannwr

④ Sgwd
yr Eira

⑤

Nedd Fechan

Pont
Melin-fach ⓐ

258 ▲

POWYS
RHONDD

Sgwd
Ddwli

Waterfall

260 ▲

Sgwd
Gwladus

Waterfall

ⓑ

0   ½ mile
0   500m

POWYS

NEATH

Craig y
Ddinas

P

A465

Pontneddfechan

White Horse
Inn

Angel PH

ⓒ

Craig y Ddinas
Hotel PH

Neath

A4109

B4242

217 ▲

Merthyr
Tydfil

1 Cross the road at the entrance to the car park and head down the left-hand of the two paths, waymarked with a yellow arrow. Ignore a right fork marked 'Access for Cavers' and follow the main path through a kissing gate and on to the river bank. Now keep the river to your right to follow a rough footpath through a couple more kissing gates to reach a footbridge.

2 Don't cross but continue ahead on the main path to climb steeply up to a fence. Stay with the path, with a wooden fence now on your right, for a few paces and you'll reach a junction of footpaths marked with a large fingerpost. Bear sharp left on to a well-surfaced track, waymarked to Gwaun Hepste, and follow this for a short distance to another junction, where you should turn right (waymarked 'Sgwd yr Eira').

3 Continue walking along the well waymarked forest trail until another fingerpost directs you right, downhill. Follow this track to the edge of the forest and then bear around to the right. This track leads to the top of a set of wooden steps, on the left.

4 Go down the 167 steps to Sgwd yr Eira (Waterfall of the Snow) and then, having edged along the bank and walked behind the falls (waterproofs recommended), retrace your steps back up to the edge of the wood. Turn left and continue, still following the redbanded posts, to a fork marked with another fingerpost.

5 Turn left here (waymarked to Sgwd y Pannwr) and descend to the riverside. Turn left again to Sgwd y Pannwr (Fullers Falls), then turn around to walk upstream to Sgwd Clun-gwyn Isaf (Lower Waterfall of the White Meadow). Take care, the ground is very steep and rough around the best viewpoint.

6 Retrace your steps downstream to your original descent path and turn left to climb back up to the fork at the top. Turn left and follow the red-banded waymarkers along to Sgwd Clun-gwyn Isaf. From here, continue along the main trail to the place where you split off earlier.

7 Drop back down to the footbridge and continue along the river bank to Porth yr Ogof.

WHERE TO EAT AND DRINK The New Inn in the small hamlet of Ystradfellte is approximately 1 mile (1.6km) from the start and incredibly popular with walkers, cyclists and cavers.

WHAT TO SEE The river may offer rare sightings of the dipper, a dark brown bird with a white bib, slightly smaller than a blackbird. It's usually seen bobbing up and down on rocks in mid-stream.

WHILE YOU'RE THERE Porth yr Ogof is accessed by following the steps down from the rear of the car park. You can walk in far enough to see the Pool of the White Horse, named after a strip of white calcite on the wall. Legend says it formed after a princess rode her horse into the cave while evading murderous pursuers. The horse fell and she drowned. Great care is needed around the cave entrance, as a fall could be fatal.

And More Hidden Gems

DISTANCE 9.5 miles (15.3km)   **MINIMUM TIME** 5hrs

ASCENT/GRADIENT 1,180ft (360m) ▲▲▲   **LEVEL OF DIFFICULTY** +++

SEE MAP AND INFORMATION PANEL FOR WALK 23

At Point ❷, cross the footbridge and follow the path upwards through a kissing gate until it meets a gravel drive. Turn left and walk out on to the road where you turn right. Pass a small filling station and tiny old fashioned shop (it opened in the 1950s and has barely changed since) on the left and look for a stile on the left. Cross this and walk diagonally across the field to go through a gate and keep ahead to a junction with a drive.

Keep left on this and walk past a house (Heol-Fawr) and through a gate. Continue along the track around right- and left-hand bends, then look for a waymarker post showing a permissive path down to the right. Walk slightly right down the field to a gate, and then continue down the middle of the next field to another gate. Go through, and keep straight ahead to drop steeply to reach a stile above the river.

Turn left and follow the narrow path downstream, crossing a few more stiles as you go. At the road, turn right to cross the bridge and then left into the picnic area of Pont Melin-fach, Point ❹. Follow the riverside path past a number of impressive falls and rapids to a wooden footbridge on your left. Ignore this, but continue to cross another bridge directly ahead.

Once over, turn right to follow an easy path to Sgwd Gwladus (Waterfall of the Chieftain), Point ❹, then retrace your steps back to the bridge and turn right. Continue along the broad track to the road at Pontneddfechan, Point ❹. Turn left to cross the bridge and pass the White Horse Inn, then turn left again on to the road and fork right where the main road goes straight ahead towards Ystradfellte.

Follow the road to a footbridge on the right, cross this and continue to a junction with a broad, hedged track. Turn left on to this and follow it to its end, where you turn left, then right into Craig y Ddinas car park. Follow the grassy track up the left-hand side of car park. This turns into a stony path that climbs steeply above the crags.

Continue easily, keeping left at a fork with a track that drops down the fence. At the next fork, keep straight ahead, signposted 'Sgwd yr Eira', and continue along the ridge through a small conifer plantation. A waymark shows an advised path that heads right and then left around some ruins and this leads to an open grassy area at a junction of paths. Keep ahead to drop steeply down steps to the waterfall at Point ❹. Pass beneath the falls and continue on the route with Walk 23.

Overleaf: Carreg Cennen Castle, Brecon Beacons National Park (Walk 25)

Carreg Cennen Castle

DISTANCE 4 miles (6.4km)   MINIMUM TIME 2hrs

ASCENT/GRADIENT 590ft (180m) ▲▲▲   LEVEL OF DIFFICULTY ✚✚✚

PATHS Good paths and tracks

LANDSCAPE Rolling pastures, deciduous woodland, short riverside stretches

SUGGESTED MAP AA Walker's Map 18 West & Central Brecon Beacons

START/FINISH Grid reference: SN666193

DOG FRIENDLINESS Not welcome in castle grounds, most stiles not dog friendly, care needed near livestock

PARKING Car park beneath castle

PUBLIC TOILETS At start

Carreg Cennen is one of the most dramatically positioned castles in the whole of the principality. It occupies an airy perch atop precipitous limestone cliffs and commands fine views in all directions. Throughout this walk – which is marked by signposts bearing a red castle symbol – you're treated to many fleeting glimpses of the towering spectacle and then at the end you can actually explore the ruins themselves.

Unusually, Carreg Cennen was built by the Welsh rather than the Normans. The first stronghold was constructed in the late 12th century, although legend tells of a fortress here during the reign of King Arthur, controlled by Urien Rheged and his son Owain. A Roman coin found on the site suggests even earlier settlement. Just for good measure, there is meant to be a warrior asleep beneath the castle. This knight – who is possibly even King Arthur himself – will apparently arise to save Wales in the nation's hour of greatest need.

Carreg Cennen changed hands several times before it was eventually seized by Edward I in 1277. A hundred or so years later it was taken down and a new fortress built in its place by one John Giffard. However, the fortunes of the castle remained the same – changing hands at a brisk rate, with owners including John of Gaunt and Henry of Bolingbroke, who went on to become King Henry IV. It also had time to fit in a siege around 1403 during the uprising staged by Owain Glyndŵr, when it took quite a beating.

During the Wars of the Roses in the 15th century, the castle's owners sided with the Lancastrians. This proved a bad decision and, after the eventual Yorkist victory in 1461, the castle was demolished by 500 local men who were paid £28 between them to complete the task.

A thrilling feature of the castle is a limestone cave that can be reached down a set of steps. The passageway is lined with stone and the ceiling of the cave is vaulted with a dovecote built into a wall. Do remember to take along a torch if you want to explore the cave.

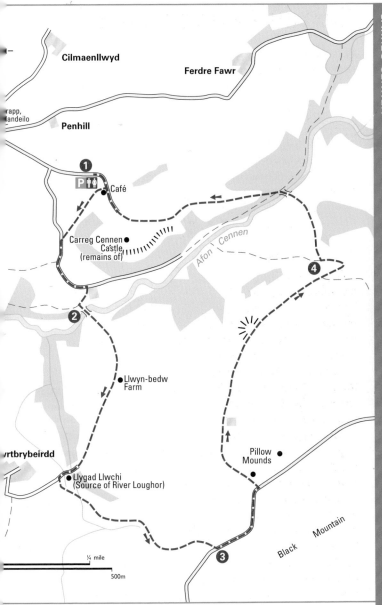

Cilmaenllwyd

Ferdre Fawr

rapp,
andeilo

Penhill

1

P 🚻 ● Café

Carreg Cennen ●
Castle
(remains of)

Afon Cennen

2

4

● Llwyn-bedw
Farm

rtbrybeirdd

● Llygad Llwchi
(Source of River Loughor)

Pillow ●
Mounds
●

Black   Mountain

3

¼ mile

500m

1 From the car park, head out of the gate at the top and proceed towards the castle. As you reach the part-white building on the right, turn right through a gate on to a footpath. Follow this diagonally leftwards, down to join the fence on the left-hand side of the field and

down to a kissing gate that leads on to a road. Turn left and pass a footpath on your right to head around a left-hand bend. Before you reach the house on the right, turn right through a gate and walk down the centre of the field to a stile. Cross this to drop steeply down to another stile and across the field to a footbridge over the River Cennen.

2 Cross the bridge and climb steeply up towards the left-hand hedge where you cross an iron stile. Continue upwards, along the fence, to the top of the field where you bear right to follow it around, beneath Llwyn Bedw farm. This leads to an opening where you join an obvious farm track and bear right. Follow this across a cattle grid and over a shallow ford to another cattle grid. Climb up a short hill and, at the top, turn left over a stile. Follow the edge of the field and climb a stile. Cross the small stream and bear right up a stony track to a stile. Cross this, then the adjacent stile by the caving notice, to follow a narrow path down to the source of the River Loughor. This is an enchanted spot with the infant river gushing to freedom from the cave that imprisoned it for the formative stages of its life. The limestone landscape in this area of the Black Mountain is peppered with sinkholes and caves similar to this one. Return to the two stiles and turn right, back on to the footpath, to continue past a ruined lime kiln on the left. Follow the track up and around to the left where it peters out into open pasture.

Continue straight ahead between two huge dips in the ground to a stile, then bear half right, keeping a fenced-off shake hole to the left, to a stile and a narrow road.

3 Turn left and follow the road up over a cattle grid and around a left-hand bend. As the road swings right, turn left on to a clear farm track. Continue to where the drive bears right to the house and keep straight ahead, over a stile and alongside a grove of ash trees for 200yds (182m) to a gate. Turn right and follow the fenced path up the hillside. The views of the castle from here are among the best on the walk. Continue through a gate and then a stile and along a sunken path to join a stony track on a hairpin bend. Keep ahead (downhill) to another hairpin bend and round this then turn right, over a stile, to drop to a stream.

4 Bear left on the bank and cross a stile, a footbridge and another stile. This leads to a larger footbridge over the River Cennen. Turn right, then left on to a waymarked path that climbs up through oak trees towards the castle. From the entrance, follow the tarmac track down to the car park.

WHERE TO EAT AND DRINK The cafe by the car park is the only place for refreshment on the walk, but this does serve up some great local home-cooked food. If you'd prefer a licensed establishment then head for nearby Trapp, a few miles west of the castle, where the rustic Cennen Arms keeps good beer and serves good food.

WHAT TO SEE At the far end of the walk, the huge banks of earth and rock on the right are Pillow Mounds. These are thought to be the remains of a Bronze Age burial site, although another line of thought suggests that they could be commercially farmed rabbit warrens, a common practice in Victorian times.

WHILE YOU'RE THERE Take a look at the colourful Georgian houses and 19th-century stone bridge over the River Tywi in the market town of Llandeilo, the ancient capital of West Wales.

The Escarpments of the Carmarthen Fan

DISTANCE 7.5 miles (12.1km)   **MINIMUM TIME** 4hrs 30min

ASCENT/GRADIENT 2000ft (610m) ▲▲▲   **LEVEL OF DIFFICULTY** +++

PATHS Faint paths, trackless sections over open moorland

LANDSCAPE Imposing mountains, hidden lakes, wild and remote moorland

SUGGESTED MAP AA Walker's Map 18 West & Central Brecon Beacons

START/FINISH Grid reference: SN798238

DOG FRIENDLINESS Care needed near livestock and steep drops

PARKING At end of small unclassified road, southeast of Llanddeusant

PUBLIC TOILETS None on route

NOTES Best not undertaken in poor visibility

The view eastwards from the flanks of Bannau Sir Gaer across Llyn y Fan Fach to the steepest section of the Carmarthen Fan is breathtaking. There's something special about the broody black waters, their shimmering surface reflecting skywards a rippled mirror image of the shattered crags of the escarpment. Ravens, buzzards and red kites ride high on the updraughts and the picture becomes all the more sinister for the addition of a little light cloud, drifting in and out of the summits.

THE LADY OF THE LAKE

You won't be the first to become bewitched by this lavish scene. The lake was visited regularly long ago by a local shepherd boy known as Rhiwallon. He encountered a mystical lady, as beautiful as the reflection in the lake that she'd risen from. Her wisdom matched her beauty and she possessed the ability to make healing potions from herbs and flowers. Rhiwallon was captivated, so much so that he proposed marriage and she agreed, but only on the condition that he should never strike her with iron. Rhiwallon and his wife had a son before the inevitable happened, perhaps by accident, and the lady returned to the dark waters, taking with her all of their worldly goods, including the animals they tended. Fortunately, before she left, she had passed on all of her medicinal skills to her son, who went on to become a local healer. Far fetched? Maybe, but it's perhaps possible to see where the roots of the tale lie. The encroachment of the Iron Age would have certainly been treated with some suspicion by the local population. Much later on, the area did actually become renowned for its healers and there followed a long line of successful practitioners known as the Physicians of Myddfai (a small village north of the lake).

26

CARMARTHEN FAN

From the narrow summit of Fan Foel, your grapple with gravity is rewarded by huge views across the bleak uplands of the Black Mountain (singular), not to be confused with the Black Mountains (plural) which are some 30 miles (48km) east of here and visible on a clear day. This is the westernmost mountain range of the National Park and, without doubt, the wildest and most remote. The majority of the land is made up of barren, windswept moorland that possesses an austere beauty with few equals. Unusually, a large percentage is actually owned by the National Park Authority.

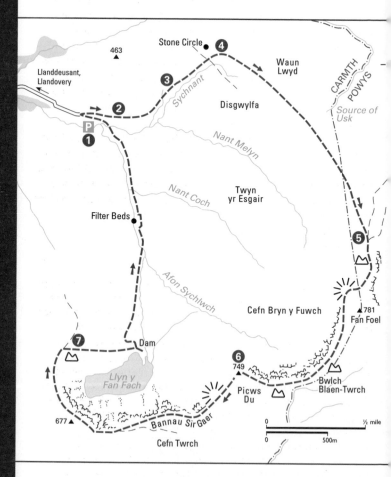

❶ From the car park at the end of the unclassified road, head back towards Llanddeusant and after about 100yds (91m) turn sharp right, almost doubling back on yourself, to continue on a faint track that contours eastwards around the hillside. Follow this track as it then veers northeast into the small valley carved out over the centuries by the Sychnant brook.

❷ The track becomes clearer, briefly. However, it is very easy to be seduced into surging up to the east here along the much more obvious valley of Nant Melyn. It's very important not to be

88

fooled but to keep to the left bank of the smaller Sychnant which turns to the northeast.

3 The track is faint but the going reasonably easy as you continue up the valley, crossing a small tributary and following the bank above the Sychnant. Numerous paths and sheep tracks cross your way, but continue unhindered upwards, aiming for the shallow saddle on the blunt ridge above. The stream eventually swings to the right and peters out. At this stage, bear right and head along the ridge.

4 You're now aiming for the steep and obvious spur of Fan Foel, which lies southeast of you, approximately 1.5 miles (2.4km) away. Follow whatever tracks you can find over Waun Lwyd and, as the ridge starts to narrow, keep to the crest where you'll meet a path coming up from the northeast.

5 Climb steeply up the narrow path on to the escarpment and keep right to follow the escarpment along. The path becomes clearer as it drops steeply into Bwlch Blaen-Twrch. From here, climb up on to Bannau Sir Gaer and continue to the summit cairn.

6 Stay with the main footpath and follow the edge of the escarpment above the precipitous cliffs into a small saddle or col and up again above Llyn y Fan Fach. Continue around the lake, with the steep drop to your right and you'll see a good path dropping down a grassy spur to the outflow of the lake.

7 Follow this obvious footpath and then, when you reach the dam, pick up the well-surfaced track that heads back downhill. This will lead you to the right of the waterworks filter beds and back to the car park.

WHERE TO EAT AND DRINK The Red Kite (formerly the Cross Inn pub) has been re-fitted as a cafe, restaurant and gift shop and now serves hot drinks and home-cooked light meals. As its name suggests, it's right next to the Red Kite Feeding Centre – tickets for the centre can be purchased at the cafe.

WHAT TO SEE To the south of the escarpment, the old red sandstone which acts as a spine for most of the high ground in the Brecon Beacons, slips beneath a layer of much younger limestone. The distinctive light-coloured outcrops can easily be seen from this walk, especially looking southeast from the summit of Bannau Sir Gaer. Look closer for the potholes and caves that typify this environment - the suggested Ordnance Survey map for this area shows that it is pockmarked all the way to the Tawe Valley.

WHILE YOU'RE THERE The Dan-yr-Ogof Showcaves, on the A4067 near Glyntawe, are approximately 10 miles (16km) from the start of the walk. Claiming to be the largest cave system in Europe, the huge caverns are certainly spectacular. There are no guided tours, you simply walk yourself around, following a clear path between the stalactites and stalagmites, while listening to a recorded commentary. Other attractions on the site include a dinosaur park, Iron Age farm, a museum, shire horse centre and a covered children's play area. Open April to October, daily from 10am, as well as during December for a Father Christmas experience and during February half-term.

Walking the Welsh Uplands

DISTANCE 9.5 miles (15.3km)		**MINIMUM TIME** 6hrs	

ASCENT/GRADIENT 2000ft (610m) ▲▲▲   **LEVEL OF DIFFICULTY** +++

PATHS Riverside path, faint or non-existent paths over moorland, some good tracks, some awkward stream crossings

LANDSCAPE Stunning valley, remote moorland, some forestry

SUGGESTED MAP OS Explorer 200 Llandrindod Wells & Elan Valley

START/FINISH Grid reference: SN860530

DOG FRIENDLINESS Care needed near livestock

PARKING Car park northeast of Abergwesyn

PUBLIC TOILETS At start

NOTES Difficult navigation, avoid in poor visibility

This is the toughest walk in the whole book, but more by the nature of the terrain than the amount of ascent. The rewards, for those who are prepared to navigate their way carefully over one short stretch of trackless moorland, are rich beyond description, for this is a foray into the wilder side of Wales – a place that sees few footprints. For less experienced walkers, this is definitely one to tackle only after you've cut your teeth on the high ground of the Brecon Beacons, and then only in good visibility. Alternatively, if you're unsure about the navigation, or if you are in any doubt about the visibility, follow the outward leg on to Drygarn Fawr and return by retracing your steps.

The remote nature of the landscape links this area, more than any other, with one of Britain's most beautiful birds, the red kite. It was the scene of this most majestic raptor's final stand. Free of persecution, pesticides and disturbance, a mere handful defiantly resisted extinction by scavenging these moors and nesting in the abundance of trees that line the valleys. Their decline was thankfully halted by a number of conservation groups who, working closely with local landowners, started a release programme of birds imported from Scandinavia and Spain. Successful breeding in both England and Scotland began in 1992 and since then the population has increased so significantly they are almost common here today.

SPOTTER'S GUIDE

The birds are easily distinguished from the more common buzzard, which can also be seen in this area, as they are much slimmer in build with narrower, more angular wings and a distinct fork in the longer tail. The plumage is a mixture of russet red and chestnut brown with white wing patches and a silver head. Their flight is more agile and a close view will show the tail constantly twisting as if trimming a sail.

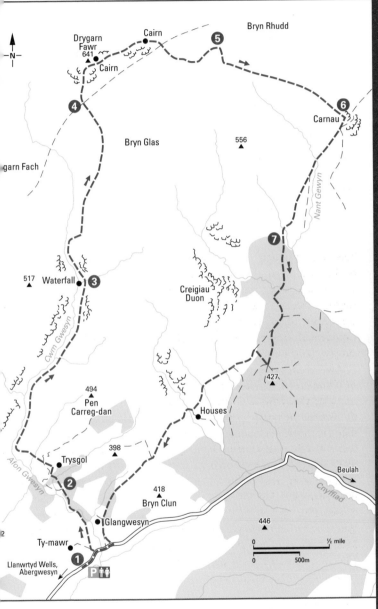

① Turn right on to the road and walk up to the bridge, just before which a stony track heads up left. Take this and after 100yds (91m) turn right,

through a gate. Follow the track across fields and down to the Afon Gwesyn, which you ford. Continue to a gate and up towards a wood where the track splits. Choose the top option and then, as this bends around to the left and heads downhill 20yds (18m) later, fork right, to traverse the clearing to a gap in the wood.

2 Follow the path down to a ford. Climb on to open ground and bear right to climb to a farm track by some buildings. Turn left on to this and follow it through a gate, where you fork left to walk beneath some crags. Ignore another fork to the left and continue to open ground. Follow the east side of the valley for over 1.5 miles (2.4km) to a waterfall.

3 Pass this to the right, then continue until the path almost disappears. Follow the line of the stream until you reach a distinctive small ridge coming in from the right. Take this uphill for 150yds (135m) and then bear left on to a narrow path, which leads you around a number of boggy patches until the cairned summit of Drygarn Fawr becomes visible. The path is often very indistinct. If you become unsure, aim for the crags and use a compass.

4 Climb the grassy slope to the trig point, then follow the ridge east past both cairns. A close scan of the hillsides to the east-southeast should reveal two grassy tops, 1.5 miles (2.4km) away, one with a large cairn on top – this is Carnau, your next objective. A clear grassy track descends east from the cairn. Follow this until it levels completely and rounds a left-hand bend, where you'll make out a faint path forking right. This is the start of the careful navigation and if you're in any doubt about visibility, you will be better off turning around and retracing your tracks.

5 Follow the track to the left of a solitary boundary marker. Turn sharp right here (south), away from the path, and cross wet ground to climb slightly on to a very broad rounded ridge. Notice the head of a small valley ahead and, as you drop into this, bear slightly left to follow the high ground with the valley to your right. Continue on sheep tracks to cross a couple of hollows, until you reach a grassy hilltop on your left. From here, you should be able to see the cairn ahead. Take the clear path that leads to it. Alternatively, keep as straight a line as you can from the cairn, with your eyes fixed on Carnau and your compass to the fore.

6 From Carnau you'll see the start of a clear gorge away to the southwest. Walk towards this, on a visible path, and join a good track as you cross the river. Continue downstream on the far bank and then stay with the path as it bears away right and crosses open hillsides. Take a right when the path forks in order to drop into the bottom of the valley, where you need to ford the stream to go through a gate.

7 Climb on a good track that eventually drops to cross another stream via a footbridge and then continue up to a five-way junction. Turn sharp right here, go through a gate and then another on the left. Drop down through the field past a sheepfold and through three gates and on to an enclosed track and follow this to a junction above some houses on your left. Keep right, going onto a grassy path, cross a stream and then take the track across a field to a path junction. By a cluster of gates, go through three to keep straight ahead and descend through the yard of Glangwesyn to the road. Turn right on to the road to return to your car.

Craig Cerrig–Gleisiad Nature Reserve

DISTANCE 4 miles (6.4km)   MINIMUM TIME 2hrs

ASCENT/GRADIENT 1,050ft (320m) ▲▲▲   LEVEL OF DIFFICULTY ✦✦✦

PATHS Clear footpaths and broad stony tracks

LANDSCAPE Imposing crags and rolling moorland, great views

SUGGESTED MAP AA Walker's Map 18 West & Central Brecon Beacons

START/FINISH Grid reference: SN972221

DOG FRIENDLINESS Take care near livestock, on lead in nature reserve

PARKING Pull-in by small picnic area on A470, 2 miles (3.2km) north of Storey Arms

PUBLIC TOILETS Forest car park south of Storey Arms

This is a short walk but it has much to offer. Firstly, there are some fine views over the Tarell Valley to the true kings of the National Park, Pen y Fan and Corn Du, whose lofty crowns command your attention for most of the way round. And secondly, the daunting crags of Craig Cerrig-gleisiad are a true spectacle in their own right and are well worth admiring close up, both from below and above.

This unique environment hosts a range of habitats and some rare species of flora and fauna. The cirque itself was formed by the action of an Ice Age glacier, which scoured out a deep hollow in the hillside and then deposited the rocks it had accumulated at the foot of the cliff to form banks of moraine. The retreating ice left a legacy – a selection of arctic-alpine plants that were sheltered from the rising temperatures by the north-facing escarpment. These plants, which include saxifrages and roseroot, also need a lime-rich soil, present on the escarpments but not on the more acidic moorland on the tops. For most of these plants, the Brecon Beacons represent the southernmost part of their range.

The cliffs only make up a fraction of the 156-acre (63ha) National Nature Reserve. One of the things that makes Craig Cerrig-gleisiad (which means 'Blue-stone Rock') – special is the diversity of the terrain. The lower slopes are home to mixed woodland and flowers such as orchids and anemones, while the high ground supports heather and bilberry. The diversity isn't just restricted to plants either – 16 species of butterfly have been recorded on the reserve and over 80 different types of birds, including the ring ouzel, or mountain blackbird as it's often known, and the peregrine falcon, which is definitely a bird of the cliffs. This mainly upland region of the Brecon Beacons National Park is partitioned from the central Brecon Beacons by the deep slash of the Taf and Tarell valleys. The name Fforest Fawr, which means Great

Forest, comes not from trees but from its one-time status as a royal hunting ground. The north-facing escarpment, of which Craig Cerrig-gleisiad forms a part, is steep and impressive. As the land dips to the south, it is chiselled into a succession of north–south running valleys that cradle infant forms of some of the National Park's greatest rivers. These are best seen on its southern fringes, where they form Fforest Fawr's greatest spectacle, Waterfall Country.

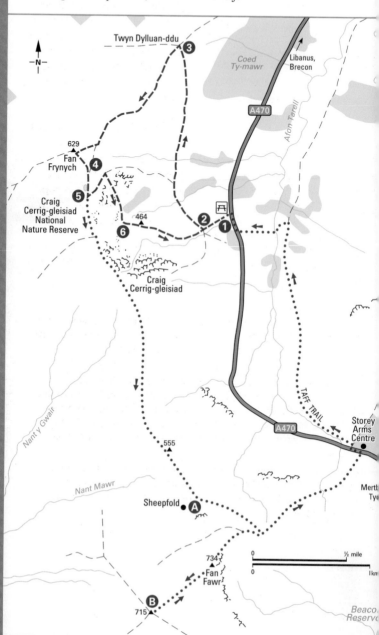

1 There's a bridge and a small picnic area at the southern end of the lay-by. Go through the kissing gate on the other side of the bridge to the picnic area. Head towards the crags, following a clear footpath, until you come to a gap in the next wall.

2 Pass through this and turn right to follow a dry-stone wall north. Head down into a small valley and cross the stream to continue in the same direction. Drop into another, steeper, valley and climb out, still following the track. Continue through the bracken to a kissing gate.

3 Cross and turn left on to a stony track. Follow this up to a gate and a stile and continue through rough ground, churned up by mining, until it levels on a dished plateau. Bear right here to the whitewashed trig point of Fan Frynych, then turn sharp left to return to the main track above the escarpment.

4 Turn right on to the main track again and continue past more rough ground before dropping slightly into a broad but shallow valley. Near the bottom, go through a kissing gate on the left (signed 'Beacons Way').

5 Follow the obvious path straight ahead and cross the top of the steep hillside to a beautifully built ice cream cone-shaped cairn. Turn right here to drop steeply all the way down into the heart of the nature reserve, following regular waymark posts.

6 As the ground levels, bear around to the right to follow a signed diversion and continue alongside the stream to the gap in the wall you passed through earlier. Go through again and follow the outward path back to the car park.

WHERE TO EAT AND DRINK The National Park Visitor Centre at Libanus serves tasty lunches, with vegetarian options, as well as delicious home-made cakes. If you fancy a pub there's the Tai'r Bull Inn, also at Libanus.

WHAT TO SEE Much of the outward leg follows the line of a pristine dry-stone wall. Although changes in farming practices in the hills haven't altered as radically as they have in many lowland areas, the hedgerows and walls that once divided the land are expensive to maintain and have been slowly replaced by wire fences. The National Park Authority provides free consultation to landowners wishing to keep the more scenic traditional crafts alive.

WHILE YOU'RE THERE This is the nearest walk to the National Park Visitor Centre on Mynydd Illtud Common, near Libanus. It's a good source of information about the National Park, hosts some great displays and has a programme of guided walks.

Into Fforest Fawr

DISTANCE 8 miles (12.9km) **MINIMUM TIME** 5hrs

ASCENT/GRADIENT 1,600ft (488m) ▲▲▲ **LEVEL OF DIFFICULTY** +++

SEE MAP AND INFORMATION PANEL FOR WALK 28

The untracked moorland of Fforest Fawr sees far fewer visitors than the mountains on the other side of the main thoroughfare. For this reason, it's always refreshing to escape the crowds and climb the highest and most accessible mountain in the range, Fan Fawr. The route across the tops from Craig Cerrig-gleisiad is a good introduction to the type of walking found in this area.

Leave Walk 28 at Point ❺ and drop to the bottom of the valley where you'll cross a stile next to a small pond before climbing back up, following the fence on your left, until you see your next objective, Fan Fawr, looming large ahead. Between you and its rounded summit lies a few miles of open moorland that typifies this part of the National Park. Continue uphill to the highest point, close to the summit of Craig Cerrig-gleisiad, then follow the line of the wall down for a few paces before bearing right on to a faint path that runs along the ridge towards Fan Fawr.

Stay with this for over a mile (1.6km), and when you reach the lowest point – a very boggy plateau directly beneath Fan Fawr – keep left to follow an even fainter path towards the right-hand end of a small crag on the steep hillside, at roughly the same height as you are. Climb to a circular sheepfold, Point Ⓐ, then bear left to walk above the small crag until you come to a slim terrace that contours around the hillside. Follow this around the eastern flank of the mountain until you eventually meet the well-trodden main track, coming up from your left. Turn right on to this and follow it steeply to the top. Continue southwest to the trig point, Point Ⓑ, and then retrace your steps back to the steep path. Drop down and cross the path you followed earlier to continue into a boggy saddle, where the path becomes harder to follow. Maintain the same direction, climbing slightly to leave the saddle, then drop easily down to a gate by the car park on the A470.

Cross the road to the Storey Arms and turn left. You'll see a track that forks off to the right (signposted 'Taff Trail'). This is the line of the old road between Merthyr Tydfil and Brecon. In those days the Storey Arms was a coaching inn. Follow the track through a couple of bands of woodland to a waymarked footpath on the left, in the corner of a wood. Take this and drop down to a footbridge that crosses the Afon Tarell. Climb the opposite bank and keep straight ahead past a large oak tree to meet the A470 again, at a stile. Turn right to return to the car park.

The Pen y Fan Pilgrimage

DISTANCE 5 miles (8km)   MINIMUM TIME 2hrs 30min

ASCENT/GRADIENT 1,610ft (491m) ▲▲▲   LEVEL OF DIFFICULTY +++

PATHS Clearly defined tracks

LANDSCAPE Rugged high mountains and deeply scooped valleys

SUGGESTED MAP AA Walker's Map 18 West & Central Brecon Beacons

START/FINISH Grid reference: SN982203

DOG FRIENDLINESS Care needed near sheep and on cliff tops

PARKING Lay-by on A470, opposite Storey Arms and telephone box

PUBLIC TOILETS 0.25 miles (400m) south of start

Every mountain has its 'trade route' – the easiest and most trafficked way to the top – and Pen y Fan is no different. At 2,907ft (886m), this is the highest peak in southern Britain and the closest real mountain to a huge chunk of the population, attracting mass pilgrimages from the English Home Counties, Birmingham, Bristol and South Wales. The most commonly used tactic is an out-and-back approach, using the motorway-like track that heads west from the southern edge of the small plantation, but this is a less rewarding walk than the simple circular route described here, which starts by crossing the head of the Taff Valley.

The geology of Pen y Fan includes a fascinating hotchpotch of rocks. Pen y Fan is composed of old red sandstone laid down during the Devonian period. The lower sections are sandstone and mudstone from the Senni Beds Formation, the stones near the top are from the Brownstones Formation, whilst the summit (and that of nearby Corn Du) are sandstones from the Plateau Beds Formation.

CORN DU

Next to Pen y Fan, and easily accessible from it across a short saddle, is Corn Du (from the Welsh for 'black horn' and pronounced corn dee). Just 43ft (13m) lower than its illustrious neighbour, it's the home of a Bronze Age burial cairn. Below it, to the northwest, is Cwm Llwch, a glacial lake, while just along the ridge towards Pen Milan is the obelisk on which is told the sad story of five-year-old Tommy Jones (see p105).

Over the years, Pen y Fan and the surrounding mountains have claimed a number of lives due to sudden bad weather. Do check the forecast beforehand and if conditions aren't favourable, don't go. On bright sunny days a trip up Pen y Fan is an unforgettable experience – on the very clearest you can see from Preseli Hills to the Black Mountains and as far south as Exmoor. However, when the weather closes in, visibility can drop to almost nothing very quickly.

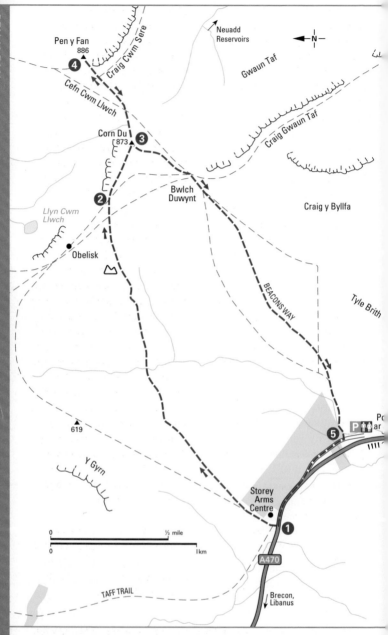

1 Cross the road and go through the gate next to the telephone box. The large building to your right is the Storey Arms, now an outdoor education centre but once a wayside inn on the coaching road between Brecon and South Wales. The original

road can be seen forking off to your left, this forms a section of the Taff Trail, a long distance route between Cardiff and Brecon. Follow a clear, in places artificial, path up the hillside, leaving the plantation behind and crossing the open moorland of the southern flanks of Y Gyrn – a rounded summit to your left. You'll soon gain the ridge and go through a kissing gate to drop easily down to the infant Taf Fawr – a pleasant and sheltered spot, ideal for a break before you reach the exposed hilltops above. The way ahead is clear, with the newly laid man-made track climbing steeply up the hillside opposite. Follow this, keeping straight ahead at a fork near the top, until it reaches the escarpment edge above the magnificent valley of Cwm Llwch. Below you'll see the glacier formed lake of Llyn Cwm Llwch, and above this the steep head wall that unites the twin peaks.

2 Turn right to follow the clear path up towards the rocky ramparts of Corn Du. The path slips easily around the craggy outcrops and leads you up to the huge cairn on top of the broad summit plateau. The views down the valley are awesome, but take care as some of the summit rocks pretty much overhang the chasm below.

3 The way to Pen y Fan is obvious from here. Drop into the shallow saddle to the east and continue easily on to the summit. This opens up a whole new vista, with the narrow ridge of Cefn Cwm Llwch acting as the dividing wall for the remote Cwm Sere, to the right as you look out.

4 The northeast face of the mountain is particularly precipitous so take care near the edges. The most enjoyable way to begin your descent is to retrace your steps across Corn Du (Point **3**) and turn left to Bwlch Duwynt, the obvious saddle between the summit and the long ridge that runs south. Alternatively, a good path runs below Corn Du, allowing easy passage with no extra height gain. To locate this, drop back into the saddle you've just crossed and fork left, beneath the grassy slope that leads to the summit. The views from this section are to the south, over the two Neuadd reservoirs. Bwlch Duwynt represents a fairly major junction of paths, but you'll easily locate the main track that forks downhill to your right, away from Corn Du. Again, sections of this track have been laid in stone in recent years to restrict the erosion caused by thousands of walkers' feet. Follow the track easily down for just over a mile (1.6km) until you see the Taf Fawr river to your right-hand side. A short diversion to your right near the bottom will reveal a great, rocky picnic spot, situated above a small waterfall. Cross the bridge over the river and go through the kissing gate into the main car park.

5 Turn right into the car park and follow it to its end where a broad dirt track takes over. Continue along the side of the plantation and cross the road to return to the start.

WHERE TO EAT AND DRINK The Tai'r Bull Inn at Libanus, on the A470 southwest of Brecon, is a fine pub with a wood-burning stove and a cosy inglenook fireplace. The selection of food is diverse and they also serve a good pint. Alternatively, try the National Park Visitor Centre also at Libanus, which has a great coffee shop (see Where To Eat and Drink, Walk 28).

WHILE YOU'RE THERE Looking north from Pen y Fan, you'll see Brecon, tucked away at the foot of the mountains. It's the largest town in the National Park and has plenty of attractions in its own right. In addition to the cathedral, there's a county museum, a military museum and a theatre.

Overleaf: The ridges of the Black Mountains and the summit of Pen y Fan (Walk 30)

The Brecon Beacons from the Neuadd Reservoirs

DISTANCE 9 miles (14.5km)	**MINIMUM TIME** 4hrs 30 min

ASCENT/GRADIENT 2,395ft (730m) ▲▲▲   **LEVEL OF DIFFICULTY** +++

PATHS Clear well-trodden paths, boggy patches, broad rocky track

LANDSCAPE Steep rocky escarpments overlooking deep U-shaped valley and two small reservoirs

SUGGESTED MAP AA Walker's Map 18 West & Central Brecon Beacons

START/FINISH Grid reference: SO038169

DOG FRIENDLINESS Care needed near livestock, several steep drops

PARKING Neuadd car park towards end of lane heading north from Pontsticill

PUBLIC TOILETS None on route

This walk represents is a fine way to visit the area's highest ground, particularly if you feel like a longer outing than Walk 30 but are afraid of over-committing yourself, as any, or all, of the big peaks can be by-passed if required. It's also an easy way to gain the tops, as it starts at an altitude over 1,300ft (396m) and, with the exception of two short but stiff sections, the climbing remains gentle to the point of being almost undetectable.

The Taf Fechan has carved itself a beautiful valley. Its grand sweeping architecture doesn't appear any the worse for the addition of the two Neuadd reservoirs. The lower reservoir, nearest the start, opened in 1884 to provide water for Merthyr Tydfil, which during the early days of the Industrial Revolution had become something of a boom town. As the iron and steel production increased, and with it the local population, demand started to outstrip supply and the valley was dammed again, this time higher up.

HIGH PEAKS

Once up, the walk cruises easily along the sandstone promenade of Graig Fan Ddu and Craig Gwaun Taf, offering great views across the magnificent cwm to the steep head of the valley, where the two highest peaks in southern Britain preside. It also rewards the walker with some tantalising glimpses of the stunning and seldom visited valley of Cwm Crew, which runs southwest from the narrowest section of the ridge at Rhiw yr Ysgyfarnog – the Slope of the Hare. The high peaks need little introduction. Their might and stature are clear from almost any viewpoint, although you may find yourself surprised by the sheer scale of the drop from the north face of Corn Du and the incomparable northeast face of Pen y Fan, which falls precipitously down over 1,000ft

(305m) to the rolling moorland of Cwm Sere below. Not so surprising are the views from the top which are magnificent and matched only by the elation of reaching the summit. Steep and rocky ground leads down from here, with the grassy flanks of Cribyn appearing much steeper than they really are up ahead. If you don't think you can manage another climb, sneak around the peak to the right, otherwise, more fine views await. This time you can gaze north over Cwm Cynwyn, as fine a natural amphitheatre as you're ever likely to see. With the peaks bagged, you'll drop into the atmospheric rocky saddle of Bwlch ar y Fan and pick up an ancient track, known locally as the 'Gap Road'.

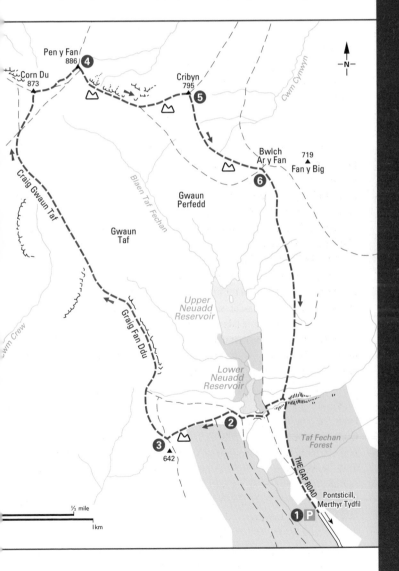

1 Leave the car park by the far end and head along the road to a gate, just before which, take a stony track the bears off to the right. Pass through a gate and over a stream in a gully before turning left at a fork to go downhill to another gate. Go through this and turn left to yet another gate. Don't go through this but turn right down a path next to it. Cross the road at the bottom, turn right and, after a few paces, turn left down a path immediately after a Neuadd Reservoir sign. This path bends down to the right of a derelict building to a small footbridge. Climb up on to the bank opposite and bear left to walk along its top. This will take you to a gate that leads out on to open moorland.

2 Go through this gate and keep straight ahead, taking the left-hand of the two tracks, which leads uphill towards the edge of a mainly felled forest. Follow the clear track up, with the forest to your left, and then climb steeply up a stony gully to the top of the escarpment.

3 Once there, turn right on to the obvious path and follow the escarpment along for over 2.5 miles (4km). You'll eventually drop into a distinct saddle with the flat-topped summit of Corn Du directly ahead. Where the path comes to a crossroads, keep straight ahead and climb easily up on to the summit. Follow the escarpment edge along and then drop down into another saddle, where you take the path up on to the next peak, Pen y Fan.

4 Again, from the summit cairn, follow the escarpment around and drop steeply, on a rocky path, down into a deep col beneath Cribyn. Keep straight ahead to climb steeply up to the cairn on the narrow summit. Note: this climb can be avoided by forking right and following another clear path that contours right around the southern flanks of the mountain and brings you out at Point **6**.

5 From the top, bear right and follow the escarpment around to the southeast. After a long flat stretch, you'll drop steeply down into to a deep col known as Bwlch Ar y Fan.

6 Turn right on to the well-made track that leads easily down the mountain. Follow this for over 1.5 miles (2.4km), until it forks. Turn left down to a stream and retrace your steps to the start.

WHERE TO EAT AND DRINK The most popular pubs in the area are at nearby Talybonton-Usk (follow the narrow lane past the beautiful Talybont Reservoir), where the pick of the bunch is the Traveller's Rest, on the outskirts of the village towards Llangynidr. This has a delightful canalside garden and a good restaurant.

WHAT TO SEE The summits of Pen y Fan, Corn Du and Cribyn were once all crowned with Bronze Age burial cairns, probably dating back to around 1800BC. It's clear that the mountains held some significance, even way back then.

WHILE YOU'RE THERE Head south to Pant, north of Merthyr Tydfil, and take a ride aboard the Brecon Mountain Railway, a narrowgauge steam train that takes a 50-minute return trip along the side of the Taf Fechan Reservoir to Dol-y-Gaer. It is great scenery and lots of fun. Open from April to October.

On the Beacons Horseshoe

DISTANCE 7 miles (11.3km)	**MINIMUM TIME** 4hrs

ASCENT/GRADIENT 2,100ft (640m) ▲▲▲   **LEVEL OF DIFFICULTY** +++

PATHS Well-defined paths and tracks, short distance on quiet lanes

LANDSCAPE Lofty peaks, angular ridges and magnificent valleys

SUGGESTED MAP AA Walker's Map 18 West & Central Brecon Beacons

START/FINISH Grid reference: SO025248

DOG FRIENDLINESS Care needed near sheep, some steep cliffs

PARKING Car park at end of small lane, 3 miles (4.8km) south of Brecon

PUBLIC TOILETS None on route

Few stories tear at the heartstrings as much as the tale of Tommy Jones. In August 1900 the five-year-old and his father were walking from the railway station in Brecon to his grandfather's farm in Cwm Llwch. They rested at the army camp at Login, where Tommy's grandfather and his 13-year-old cousin, Willie, met them. The men decided to stay a while with the soldiers but the boys continued on to the farmhouse, 0.5 miles (800m) away. As darkness fell, Tommy got scared. Willie wanted to continue to the farmhouse, but Tommy decided to return to his father. Sadly, he never made it. A huge search ensued, increasing in scale as the days went by. There were even suggestions that he'd been kidnapped or murdered. Remarkably, a few weeks later, a local woman dreamed about the boy and, although she had never been there before, led her husband up on to the ridge where they discovered Tommy's remains. A simple stone obelisk was erected close to the spot where the body was found. It was moved slightly in 1997, as the area surrounding it had become badly eroded.

SPECTACULAR ROUTE

This is far and away the most spectacular route up on to the highest ground of the National Park. The jagged ridges, steep gullies and deeply gouged valleys resemble those of the higher mountains of Snowdonia, many miles further north. The biggest climb comes early on, with a steep pull up from the car park on to the head of the lovely and remote Cwm Gwdi. The path then follows rocky, disused quarry tracks before hurdling the grassy spur that leads on to Cefn Cwm Llwch. The ridge feels incredibly airy, dividing two magnificent valleys, both cradling fast-flowing mountain streams. The rocky ramparts of the summit seem to taunt you as you continue southwards and then, as you reach the steep final step, the spectacular northeast face of Pen y Fan presents itself in its full glory. This is probably the most magnificent section of mountain scenery in the whole National Park. Steep gullies drop down from the summit, vaulting vertical crags as they plummet into the valley below, and ravens play on the ever-present updraughts. The summit, often crowded, can be an anti-climax after all the wild scenery, but it's a great mountain and there's plenty more on the descent from Corn Du. After crossing the void between the peaks, you'll trace the airy tops of Craig Cwm Llwch past the Tommy Jones obelisk, one of the Beacons' best-known landmarks. You'll then drop to a glacial lake, Llyn Cwm Llwch, an excellent picnic spot, surrounded still by the formidable walls of the head of the valley.

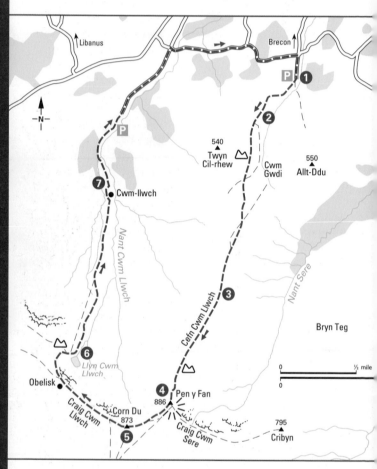

❶ Walk uphill from the car park and pass an information plinth before crossing a stile. Walk along the right-hand side of the field towards the top right-hand corner and then bear left to continue along the fence to reach another stile.

❷ Follow the broad but faint grassy track straight on. As it reaches steeper ground, it becomes a better defined stony track that swings slightly left and climbs the hillside. Continue ahead, up towards the head of Cwm Gwdi, and keep ahead, ignoring a few right forks, until the path eventually levels out on Cefn Cwm Llwch.

❸ Continue along the ridge towards the summit ahead. As you reach the foot of the peak, the track steepens considerably, offering a fine viewpoint over a perilous gully that drops into Cwm Sere on the left. Continue to climb steeply over a few rocky steps to reach the summit cairn on Pen y Fan.

❹ Bear right to follow the escarpment edge along and drop into a shallow saddle eneath the rising crest of Corn Du. Fork right up on to this summit, then bear left for a few paces to locate a steep path that drops down through rocky outcrops on to easier ground below. Bear right and drop past the summit.

❺ Continue down the hill forking right to pass the Tommy Jones obelisk with the steep crags of Craig Cwm Llwch on your right-hand side. Above

the lake, the path forks; take the right-hand option and right again at the next fork to drop steeply, around a dog-leg and over moraine banks to the lake shore.

❻ A clear track leads north from the lake – alongside the outflow; follow it over easy ground to cross a stile that leads on to a broad farm track. Take this down to a gate in front of a building and climb the stile on the left. Cross the compound and climb another stile to follow waymarker posts around to the right on to another track, beyond the building.

❼ Bear left on to this track and follow it down, over a footbridge, to a parking area. Keep straight ahead, through a gate to a crossroads, where you turn right. Cross the bridge and continue for over a mile (1.6km) ignoring turning to left to another T-junction. Turn right and walk uphill back to the car park.

WHERE TO EAT AND DRINK There's nothing close to the walk, but Brecon has plenty of choice including the scruffy but excellent value Three Horseshoes on Orchard Street, and during the summer months, the excellent Bridge Café, also on Bridge Street. Alternatively, for a cuppa and a cake, try the National Park Visitor Centre near Libanus.

WHAT TO SEE As you descend from the escarpment into Cwm Llwch, you'll drop to the shores of Llyn Cwm Llwch, a fine example of a mountain lake left behind the last ice age. As the glaciers that shaped the head of the valley retreated, the rocks and stones that they had scoured from the steep slopes were deposited at their feet creating a wall, or bank, known as a moraine. This effectively creates a dam for the lake to form.

WHILE YOU'RE THERE Hidden beneath a poverty stricken and somewhat dowdy reputation, Merthyr Tydfil is one of South Wales most fascinating towns – even its name, which was derived from the story of Tydfil, a martyred Welsh princess, is full of intrigue. The town's heyday came during the Industrial Revolution when it was the most populated town in Wales. It now boasts a great museum in the shape of Cyfartha Castle, which will certainly shed some light on a chequered and often bloody past.

Overleaf: Pen y Fan, Corn Du and the Tommy Jones obelisk (Walk 32)

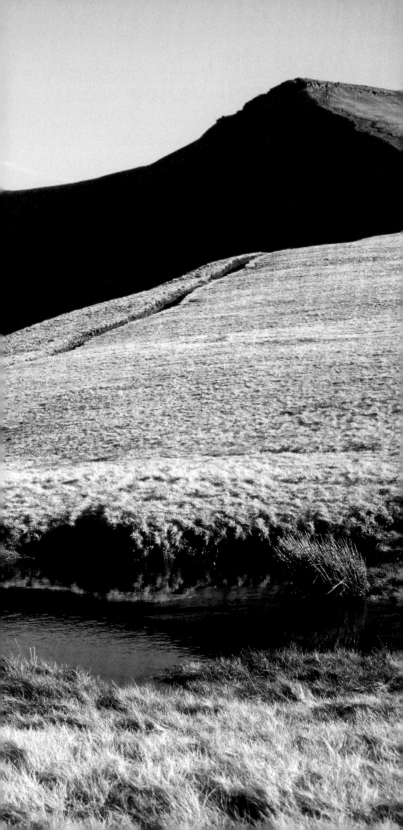

Above the Caerfanell Valley

DISTANCE 5.5 miles (8.8km)	MINIMUM TIME 3hrs 30min
ASCENT/GRADIENT 1,542ft (470m) ▲▲▲	LEVEL OF DIFFICULTY ✦✦✦

PATHS Clear tracks across open mountain tops, along river and through forest, some mud and wet peat

LANDSCAPE Moorland, craggy escarpments, remote valley, coniferous plantation, waterfalls

SUGGESTED MAP AA Walker's Map 18 West & Central Brecon Beacons

START/FINISH Grid reference: SO056175

DOG FRIENDLINESS Care needed near livestock

PARKING Large car park at start, 3 miles (4.8km) west of Talybont Reservoir

PUBLIC TOILETS None on route

This walk sums up everything that is good about walking in the Brecon Beacons. In only 5.5 miles (8.8km), it encapsulates almost every sort of landscape found in the National Park.

It starts by climbing steeply on to an impressive peak from where you track easily along a steep sandstone escarpment, so typical of the area's high mountain scenery. The airy path crosses the head of a precipitous waterfall, rubs shoulders with an expansive moorland plateau and provides views that will remain in your memory for a long time. At the halfway stage, you'll get a sneak peep of the highest peaks in the National Park as well as a bird's-eye view over Cwm Oergwm, one of the most spectacular valleys in a wild land that's famed for them. The return leg passes the forlorn wreckage of a Canadian warplane and a fitting memorial to those who perished in her, before dropping easily down to follow a delightful upland river past a series of tumbling waterfalls. It finishes with a steep pull up through a small plantation, with further cascades and rapids.

DEATH FLIGHT

As you approach the clearly visible cairn beneath Waun Rydd, a sharp eye will spot flashes of red, draped over the impeccable stonework. As you draw closer, you'll see that the red is in fact, a plethora of poppy wreaths hung over a simple memorial. A bronze plaque lists the names of the young Canadians who lost their lives when Wellington bomber R1645 came down in bad weather, following a routine training flight on 6 July 1942. The twisted wreckage, a deathly shade of dull grey, lies strewn around the bracken-covered hillside below the cairn. The serenity and beauty of the Beacons' landscape makes a fitting backdrop to the scene and it's always difficult to pass this spot without pausing for reflection.

Gigfran is Welsh for raven and the diminutive crag that shades the memorial is named after these powerful birds that can often be seen performing aerobatics above it. Ravens are synonymous with remote upland areas and rugged coastal regions, where they tend to nest on crags and feast on sheep carrion.

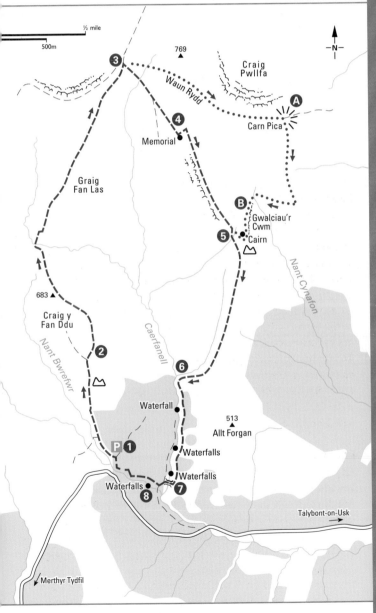

1 Walk back out of the car park, either crossing the cattle grid or a kissing gate to the left of it, then turn immediately right on to a stone track that heads uphill, with the stream on your left. Follow this track steeply up to the top of the escarpment and keep straight ahead to cross the narrow spur, where you bear around, slightly to the left, to follow the escarpment.

2 Stay on the clear path, with the escarpment to your right, for about 1.5 miles (2.4km), till you meet a number of paths at the head of the valley.

3 Take the sharp right turn to follow a narrow track slightly downwards, around the head of the valley, towards the cliffs that can be seen on the opposite hillside. Keep left at a fork and continue to the crash memorial.

4 Almost directly above the memorial, you'll see a rocky gully leading up on to the ridge. On the left-hand side of this, as you look at it, is a faint track that climbs steeply up. Take this to the top and turn right on to a narrow but clear track. Follow this track easily above the crag, to a distinctive cairn at the southern end of the ridge. Just north of the cairn you'll see a small stream.

5 Follow this down for 30ft (9m) to join a clear grassy track that trends leftwards at first, then follows a clear groove down the spur. This becomes an easy footpath that crosses a broad plateau and a bog and then leads to a junction at a wall. Turn right here and drop down to the Afon Caerfanell.

6 Cross the stile on your left at the bottom and follow the narrow footpath downstream, past a number of waterfalls. Eventually you'll pass the largest of them and arrive at a footbridge.

7 Cross the footbridge and go through a kissing gate to follow the track into the forest. Pass some ruined buildings on your right, and before you cross the small bridge, turn right on to a clear path that leads uphill into the forest with waterfalls on your left.

8 Continue uphill on the main track, crossing a stream and taking optional detours to the left and right to see other waterfalls. Eventually you'll meet a broader forest track where you turn left and climb up to a gravel path where you turn left up to the car park.

WHERE TO EAT AND DRINK Talybont-on-Usk has four pubs. The best of these is the Traveller's Rest, 500yds (457m) southeast of the village on the road to Llangynidr, which has a canalside garden and a good restaurant. There's also the Old Barn Tea Room (seasonal) a couple of miles west of the start.

WHAT TO SEE As you progress along the grassy slopes of the uplands, you'll become familiar with the sight of small, mottled brown birds that flee upon your approach. These are either skylarks or meadow pipits and although they look similar at first sighting, they can easily be told apart. The skylark is slightly larger, lighter in colour, has a stouter beak and a small crest on its head. The pipit makes a dipping flight, while the skylark is well known for its continuous song, usually performed as it hovers high above you.

The Caerfanell Valley and Carn Pica

DISTANCE 7.5 miles (12.1km)   **MINIMUM TIME** 5hrs

ASCENT/GRADIENT 1,706ft (520m) ▲▲▲   **LEVEL OF DIFFICULTY** +++

SEE MAP AND INFORMATION PANEL FOR WALK 33

This short extension crosses a broad peaty plateau to Carn Pica, a giant cairn that offers a whole new vista across the Talybont Reservoir to the Black Mountains in the distance. From here, it makes an airy skyline walk that hugs the clifftops to cross the heads of two further valleys, before rejoining Walk 33.

Leave Walk 33 at Point ❸, where you meet a number of paths at the head of the valley, and take the main track to the right. This heads slightly uphill through an area of peat hags (knolls in deep trenches). Stay on the main track, which is pretty clear on the ground, and cross the moorland plateau known as Waun Rydd. You'll locate a small cairn at the path's high point before dropping easily to a huge cairn on the escarpment edge. This is Carn Pica, Point ❹. To your left, as you look out, you'll see the cliffs of Craig Pwllfa, a perfect example of a north-facing cirque, or natural amphitheatre, carved out of the hillside by the receding glaciers of the last ice age. The grass-covered debris at its foot is known as moraine and often acts as a dam, creating glacial lakes such as Llyn Cwm Llwch (see Walk 32).

Turn right here and follow the escarpment southwards, where it steepens into significant crags. At the southern tip, you'll see a lovely narrow ridge linking the outlying summit of Allt Lwyd. Bear sharp right here to continue along the edge. The path leads to the head of a steep-sided valley, where you'll cross a small stream and bear around to the left to traverse the top of the impressive cliffs of Gwalciau'r Cwm, Point ❸. At the end of this delightful section of the route you come to a large cairn on top of a narrow spur (Point ❺).

If you don't want to visit the war memorial, which is effectively an out-and-back trip, follow Walk 33's descent instructions from here. To see the war memorial, turn right to reach the end of the steep crags, with the memorial directly below you on the left. Locate a faint grassy descent path to the north of a stony stream gully, then drop down to the cairn and wreckage. Once you've finished here, retrace your steps back to Point ❺ and continue Walk 33 to return to the car park and the end of the walk.

Around Llangorse Lake

DISTANCE 3 miles (4.8km)   MINIMUM TIME 1hr 30min

ASCENT/GRADIENT 100ft (30m) ▲ ▲ ▲   LEVEL OF DIFFICULTY ✦ ✦ ✦

PATHS Footpaths over agricultural land and short road section

LANDSCAPE Marshy lakeside surrounded by mountains

SUGGESTED MAP AA Walker's Map 17 Brecon & The Black Mountains

START/FINISH Grid reference: SO128272

DOG FRIENDLINESS Awkward stiles, care needed near livestock and wildfowl

PARKING Llangorse Lake, at start

PUBLIC TOILETS At start

NOTES In particularly wet periods the Afon Llynfi is liable to burst its banks, making the start of this walk impassable

This walk is a gentle tramp around the lush meadows that hold South Wales' largest natural lake, Llangorse. The lake perches on the watershed between the Usk to the south and the Wye, which runs north of the Black Mountains and is well known for its birdlife, which is protected by a nature reserve on the southern shores. The water attracts a huge number of wintering birds, as well as acting as a stop-off for species that migrate. The reeds lining the lake also provide an important habitat: a dragonfly known as *Ischnura pumilio*, is thought to breed only in one other spot in the UK.

On the lake, you'll find the only known crannog (manmade island) in all of Wales – and there are none at all in England. Tree-ring dating of the Llangorse crannog has established that it was put together in several stages between AD 889 and 893. However, it didn't last long, being destroyed by fire in AD 916. The Anglo Saxon Chronicle appears to reveal how this came to pass: 'Æthelflæd ['The Lady of the Mercians'] sent an army into Wales and stormed Brecenanmere [Llangorse Lake] and there captured the wife of the king and thirty-three other persons.' It's not beyond the realms of imagination that they set light to the island afterwards. Although it's not possible to visit the crannog since it is too fragile, it can be viewed by hiring a rowing boat or kayak at the lakeside and circumnavigating it. A modern replica crannog is filled with information about the crannog and the lake that surrounds it.

There are a number of tales attached to Llangorse Lake. The chronicler Giraldus Cambrensis (Gerald of Wales), who visited in 1188, wrote that local people had reported the water turning green – a portent of impending invasion – and that sometimes this phenomenon was accompanied by scarlet streaks in the water 'as if blood were flowing along certain currents and eddies' which did not bode well at all. These are now thought to have been caused by algal blooms or sediments.

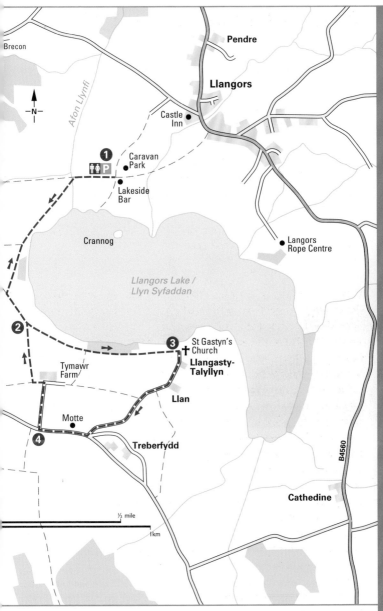

Pendre

Llangors

Brecon

Castle
Inn

Caravan
Park

❶

Lakeside
Bar

Crannog

Langors
Rope Centre

*Llangors Lake /
Llyn Syfaddan*

❷

St Gastyn's
Church

❸

**Llangasty-
Talyllyn**

Tymawr
Farm

Llan

Motte

❹

Treberfydd

B4560

Cathedine

½ mile

1km

❶ From the car park next to the public toilets, walk across the access road and continue straight across the Common on a grassy track. This leads to a small footbridge over the Afon Llynfi. Cross the bridge and bear diagonally left to cross the centre of the field towards another small footbridge and stile. Although you are obviously on level ground, the walk is blessed with great views over some of the surrounding peaks and on this stretch you'll see the sloping table top of Pen y Fan clearly ahead in the distance. Continue in the same direction across the next field until you come to a stone wall, which is vaulted by a step stile. Cross this and maintain the same direction. You'll notice a small copse on your left-hand side and beyond this a dense patch of reeds. At the end of this field, you come to a wooden footbridge. Cross this and the stile to continue in the same direction again. This leads on to a short boardwalk that takes you through a small gate. Keep straight ahead here, to the left-hand edge of the field.

2 Pass through another gate to continue along the same line. At the end of this field, pass through another gate and join a broad grassy track at a junction. This is Llangasty Nature Reserve and if you turn left here, you'll come to a hide on your left-hand side. To continue, keep straight ahead, passing through a wide gate with two waymarkers on it. Keep left to walk above a small wood and then, at the end of the wood, bear around to the left on another boardwalk, which leads you to a kissing gate. Go into the wood and cross a footbridge to continue to another kissing gate. Keep ahead here, along the bottom of the field to another gate and maintain

your direction to run along a really scenic section of the lake shore - this is a great place to take a break. After passing a few lofty Scots pines you reach yet another gate, by the elegant 19th-century church of St Gastyn's. This, along with the nearby school and manor house, was built by Robert Raikes, the originator of the Sunday School in Britain.

3 Turn right on to the lane and continue past the school (Hen Ysgol) and manor house to reach a T-junction. Turn right and continue to a footpath on the right.

4 This is signposted 'Calch Ty-Mawr'. Follow the track down towards the farm and bear left, over a stile next to a gate, immediately before the buildings. Continue along the hedge and turn right through a gate. Head down the left-hand edge of the field, passing through two gates, on either side of a track, and carry on in the same direction. At the bottom of the field, you'll come to your outward route where you turn left, through a gate, and retrace your steps back to the lakeside.

WHERE TO EAT AND DRINK There's a seasonal cafe and bar at the Lakeside Caravan Park, near the start of the walk, but if you crave really good food and drink, pop in to the excellent Castle Inn in Llangorse village, which is situated north of the lake on the B4560.

WHAT TO SEE From the lake edge you'll see a small artificial island or crannog. There's long been a myth telling of a submerged village beneath the lake and some have even told of hearing a church bell ring beneath the water. While this may be far-fetched, the lakeside was certainly inhabited by Iron Age Celts, and a dugout canoe found in the lake is displayed in the County Museum in Brecon.

WHILE YOU'RE THERE At Llangorse Multi Activity Centre on the village outskirts you can go skytrekking (think zip wires), horse-riding, BMXing, climbing or get muddy on the dingle scramble.

The Crest of Y Grib

DISTANCE 8 miles (12.9km)	**MINIMUM TIME** 4hrs 30min

ASCENT/GRADIENT 1,906ft (581m) ▲▲▲ **LEVEL OF DIFFICULTY** +++

PATHS Clear tracks over farmland, rolling moorland and narrow ridge, quiet lane

LANDSCAPE High mountain plateau, narrow ridge, steep grassy escarpment, deep and remote cwms

SUGGESTED MAP AA Walker's Map 17 Brecon & The Black Mountains

START/FINISH Grid reference: SO175295

DOG FRIENDLINESS Care needed near livestock

PARKING Castle Inn, Pengenffordd, allows parking for small fee

PUBLIC TOILETS None on route

This is the classic climb on to the highest ground of the Black Mountains. The steep western slopes of the towering massif, accentuated by a succession of grassy arêtes and rounded promontories, hide a multitude of remote cwms that rarely reveal their splendour to the walker.

Y GRIB

From the airy ramparts of Castell Dinas, the full length of the bold escarpment unfolds and, while many paths breach its defences, none do so in quite such a dramatic fashion as the one that traces the slender crest of Y Grib. Compared to the gentle standards of this normally rounded and uniform landscape, this narrow grassy walkway feels almost knife-edge in places. Once up, you'll make easy progress through the eroded peat of Pen y Manllwyn and across the top of the boggy plateau to the massif's high point of Waun Fach.

WAUN FACH

The line of descent harbours its own treasures as it follows the narrow spur of Pen Trumau, which sweeps gracefully around a deep chasm formed by the infant Grwyne Fechan river. Huge views across the valley show the formidable bulk of Waun Fach as it would want to be seen; the usually understated summit transforms itself into an impressive towering giant that stands head and shoulders above the line of pretenders to its grassy crown. A rocky saddle, steeped in the atmosphere of the craggy peaks that surround it, marks the last of the high mountain scenery.

A basic windbreak offers shelter from the cruel wind that often sweeps through the pass and also affords fine views over the expansive Grwyne Fechan Valley. The route is for more experienced walkers, and should be not attempted in poor weather or when visibility is reduced.

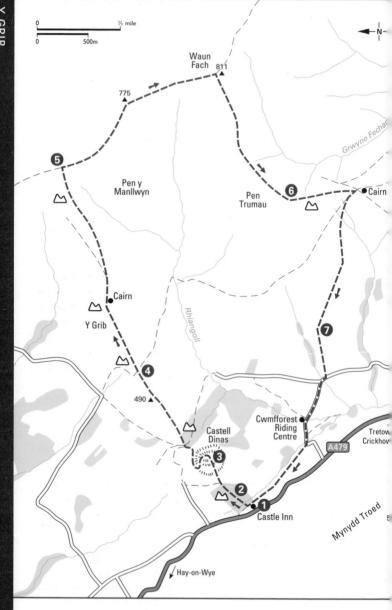

0 ½ mile
0 500m

—N—

Waun
Fach
811

775

5

Pen y
Manllwyn

Pen
Trumau

6

Cairn

Grwyne Fechan

Cairn

Y Grib

Rhiangoll

4

490 ▲

Castell
Dinas

7

Cwmfforest
Riding
Centre

Tretow
Crickhov

A479

3

2

1

Castle Inn

Mynydd Troed

Hay-on-Wye

❶ A set of wooden steps go down from the back of the car park on the eastern side of the road. These lead on to a rough track where you turn right and then, after 30yds (27m), left over a stile. Follow the permissive path down the side of the wood to a stream, cross a stile and then cross the stream.

❷ Keep to the left edge of the field, with trees on your left, and climb steeply to the top of the field. Leave the wood behind and follow the fence line upwards to another stile. This leads on to the flanks of Castell Dinas.

3 Keep straight ahead here to cross the ruins and descend steeply into a deep saddle. Cross a stile and a broad track, then climb directly up the steep spur ahead. You're now on Y Grib and it's possible to follow the faint track all the way up to a cairn and then down to a small notch where your route is crossed by a bridleway.

4 Climb steeply back out of this and hug the crest up to another cairn. Now keep ahead on a fainter path that passes another cairn before climbing steeply, straight ahead, on to the broad spur of Pen y Manllwyn.

5 Here, at a tiny cairn, turn right on to a clear track that leads over the top of Pen y Manllwyn (marked by a cairn) and up to the boggy plateau on top of Waun Fach. The summit is stranded in a puddle of wet peat that makes it an undesirable picnic spot. Turn right and follow the obvious path down on to the ever-narrowing spur of Pen Trumau.

6 Cross the narrow summit and, as the ground steepens, follow the path through rocky outcrops to a broad saddle, marked by a large cairn. Turn sharp right here and follow the main track as it descends, easily at first. This steepens and becomes rocky for a while, going through several gates, before it reaches a gate above a walled track.

7 Follow the track down to the road and turn right, then immediately left. Drop to the bottom of the valley past Cwmfforest Riding Centre and climb out again on the other side. As the road turns sharply to the left, bear right on to a stony farm track that runs between hedgerows. Follow this track until it turns sharply left where you continue straight ahead along a narrower track between hedges. This will take you past the stile you crossed earlier, on the right-hand side, then take the steps on your left, back to the car park.

WHERE TO EAT AND DRINK The Castle Inn has long been a centre for walkers, serving great food and a choice of ales. Dogs are not allowed inside, but there is a special children's menu and extra large portions are available for hungry hikers. The inn also offers bed and breakfast and low-cost bunkhouse accommodation for groups.

WHAT TO SEE At 1,476ft (450m) above sea level, Castell Dinas was one of the highest castles in Britain. Sadly, only a few stones, remain, scattered around the rocky hilltop. The Norman motte-and-bailey style castle was constructed on the site of an Iron Age settlement – the original ramparts date back around 2,500 years. It's a stunning viewpoint and, courtesy of the recently instated permissive path that leads from Pengenffordd to its crown, it adds considerable interest to this excellent high mountain walk.

WHILE YOU'RE THERE The Normans finally settled on Tretower for their best defence of the pass and in the 13th century built a basic round tower on the site of an earlier fortification. It nearly fell to both Llywelyn the Last in the late 13th century and again to Owain Glyndwr early in the 14th century. The original tower, together with a 15th-century mansion built during more peaceful times and some glorious gardens, are all open to the public.

Waun Fach from the Grwyn Fawr Valley

DISTANCE 9.25 miles (14.9km)	**MINIMUM TIME** 4hrs

ASCENT/GRADIENT 2,000ft (610m) ▲▲▲   **LEVEL OF DIFFICULTY** +++

PATHS Clear tracks over open moorland, one indistinct path over boggy ground, steep descent

LANDSCAPE Rolling moorland, deep valleys

SUGGESTED MAP AA Walker's Map 17 Brecon & The Black Mountains

START/FINISH Grid reference: SO252284

DOG FRIENDLINESS Care needed near sheep

PARKING Car park at head of lane at start

PUBLIC TOILETS None on route

NOTES Difficult navigation in poor visibility

The high ground of the Black Mountains consists of a 1-mile (1.6km) long, blunt and boggy ridge that runs between the two high points of Waun Fach and Pen y Gadair Fawr. Waun Fach sneaks the gold medal for altitude; at 2,661ft (811m), it stands a less than obvious 36ft (11m) above its shapelier neighbour. But erosion and time has reduced its lofty summit plateau to little more than a shallow peaty scoop that houses the stranded base of a long removed triangulation pillar. This has left the distinctive, conical summit of Pen y Gadair Fawr as the far more worthwhile objective. It's dry, offers great views over the Grwyne Fechan Valley and even comes complete with a tumbledown windbreak, next to the summit cairn.

The real beauty of this small cluster of rounded peaks are the valleys that drop away dramatically to either side of the ridge. The Grwyne Fechan Valley, on the western side, is the wilder and more picturesque of the two. It has no road access and its tiny brook is almost permanently in the shadow of the string of imposing peaks that define its western banks. The valley of Grwyne Fawr is the larger however (Fawr means large or great). Its windswept rolling moorland cradles a large reservoir that provides a scenic focal point for walkers and sightseers alike. It's fed by the tumbling Grwyne Fawr river, a typical fast-flowing mountain stream that rises out of the boggy plateau at its head. The easy angle of the valley means that its grassy floor, penetrated by a good track for most of its length, offers a gentle knee-up on to the higher ground and this provides the easiest approach to most of the surrounding peaks. Lower down the valley, beneath the reservoir, the walls steepen and their wooded slopes provide a short but extremely sharp exit from the lofty flanks of Pen y Gadair Fawr.

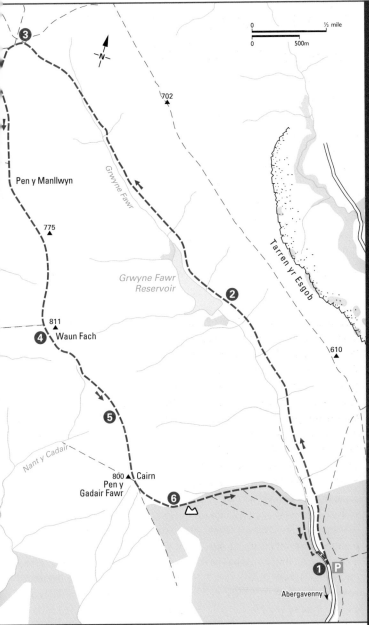

❶ Take the broad track at the far end of the car park and follow it out on to the road. Turn right to continue up the valley then, after about 30yds (27m), fork right on to a stony track that runs along the bottom of the forest. Follow this track ignoring fork off to right and continue through two gates to a third gate, by a stand of trees, situated above the Grwyne Fawr Reservoir.

❷ Keeping the trees to your left, carry on past the reservoir and up the valley. Go through another gate and continue until the track finally fords the Grwyne Fawr stream. Stay on the stony track, which now peters out to become grassy for a while before deepening into an obvious rut. Continue on to the flat ground above the steep northern escarpment, where the path meets a fence by a stile on your right.

3 Turn left on to a clear track and then, after 100yds (91m), turn left again by a tiny cairn on to a faint grassy track that leads up the front of a blunt spur. Follow this over numerous peaty hollows to the summit plateau of Waun Fach, easily identified by a large concrete block.

4 Continue on in the same direction (southeast) across a large expanse of boggy ground. There's no clear path on this section, but there are usually plenty of footprints in the wet ground leading towards the obvious cairn topped peak of Pen y Gadair Fawr, at the far end of the ridge. In the saddle between the two summits, you'll pick up a faint path that initially follows the eroded line of a stream.

5 The path improves as it continues, eventually leaving the stream behind and making a beeline for the peak ahead. Climb to the cairn, then continue in the same direction to drop steeply. Here you are faced with a plethora of unhelpfully brief paths vying for your attention. Take one of the middle ones, heading southeast towards what was the edge of the forest. Most of the trees have been harvested here, leaving rows of stumps. Make your way to the fence at the edge of the forested area and turn left along it.

6 Take particular care here because the path drops precipitously down the hillside as it hugs the fence to its right. The path follows the fence all the way down to the river, crossing a stream on the way. At the river, turn right. Continue along the river bank for about 400yds (366m), then cross the bridge to the road. Turn right on to this to return to the car park.

WHERE TO EAT AND DRINK This is a pretty remote area but the Skirrid Mountain Inn, in Llanvihangel Crucorney, just off the A465, between Abergavenny and Hereford, is reputed to be the oldest pub in Wales and is certainly worth a visit for a drink or a meal. Alternatively, head back down the A465 to Abergavenny where there's plenty of choice.

WHAT TO SEE On the trudge up to Waun Fach, you'll pass a succession of deep trenches in the grass-topped peat. These are known as peat hags and appear all over the National Park. Peat is formed where vegetable matter has decayed and broken down in a particularly wet environment. Starved of oxygen, the bacteria that are required for proper decomposition can't exist so a jelly-like substance is formed. The surfaces of these bogs are easily eroded and the action of running water combined with frost, ice, snow and very high winds has carved out deep trenches up to 10ft (3m) deep. The acidic nature of this type of soil supports a variety of plant life including heather and bilberry.

The Skyline of Crickhowell

DISTANCE 8.5 miles (13.7km) **MINIMUM TIME** 4hrs 30min

ASCENT/GRADIENT 1,700ft (518m) ▲▲▲ **LEVEL OF DIFFICULTY** +++

PATHS Waymarked footpaths, clear tracks

LANDSCAPE Grassy moorland topped with formidable peaks offering great views over deep and remote valleys

SUGGESTED MAP AA Walker's Map 17 Brecon & The Black Mountains

START/FINISH Grid reference: SO234228

DOG FRIENDLINESS Care needed near livestock, awkward stiles

PARKING Car park beneath small crag and next to bridge, in narrow lane running north from Crickhowell

PUBLIC TOILETS None on route

This walk climbs on to Table Mountain, which is topped with the remains of a fortress. It then scales the steep escarpment above to cross Pen Cerrig-calch, the highest limestone peak in the National Park. Following a superb lofty traverse that bags another formidable peak, Pen Allt-mawr, it descends a broad ridge that forms the western wall of the remote Grwyne Fechan Valley.

Towering above the mountain hub of Crickhowell, Table Mountain appears as a flat-topped knoll tucked beneath the white screes of Pen Cerrig-calch. It is topped by the ramparts of an impressive Iron Age fort known as Crug Hywel, which translates to 'Hywel's Fort.' Hywel was a significant figure in Welsh history in the 10th century. The grandson of Rhodri the Great, who killed the leader of the Viking invaders at Anglesey, he made huge strides towards the unification of the infant nation and also gained much acclaim for the introduction of a system of rules, which became known as the Law of Wales. The rules, aimed at freeing the common man from the scruples of rich and powerful merchants, gave improved rights to women as well as placing values on everyday items such as domestic cats. He became known as Hywel Dda, or Hywel the Good. Although Hywel reigned in the 10th century, the fortifications on the hilltop are probably 1,000 years older. He may have taken advantage of the naturally defended position at some stage.

PEN CERRIG-CALCH

Standing guard over Crug Hywel is the 2,300ft (701m) peak of Pen Cerrig-calch. It is unique as the highest limestone peak in a landscape that comprises mainly old red sandstone. The name says it all; *cerrig* is stone and *calch* is lime. Although it appears now to be an isolated pocket of the soft white rock, it would have once been linked to the larger tract south of the Usk.

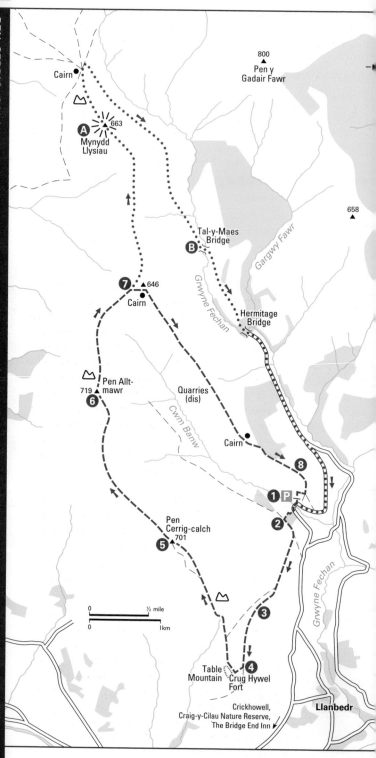

800 ▲
Pen y
Gadair Fawr

658 ▲

Cairn ●

A ☀ 663
Mynydd
Llysiau

Tal-y-Maes
Bridge
B

Gargwy Fawr

Gwyne Fechan

Hermitage
Bridge

7 ▲646
Cairn ●

Pen Allt-
mawr
719 ▲ 6

Quarries
(dis)

Cwm Banw

Cairn ●

8

1 P

2

Pen
Cerrig-calch
701
5 ▲

Gwyne Fechan

0   ½ mile
0   1km

3

Table
Mountain
4
Crug Hywel
Fort

Crickhowell,
Craig-y-Cilau Nature Reserve,
The Bridge End Inn

Llanbedr

1 Walk back over the bridge and bear right up the ramp that leads to the second gate on the right. Cross the stile up some steps to the right of the gate and walk up the edge of a field to another stile that leads on to a lane. Cross this and climb over another stile to continue, with a wood on your left, up to yet another stile in a dry-stone wall.

2 Cross this and turn left to follow a faint path around the hillside through the bracken. Walk alongside the wall to a clear offset crossroads, where the wall drops away, keep straight ahead here and at the next crossroads rejoin the wall shortly. Continue straight across another section where the wall drops away and then joins the path again.

3 Next time the wall drops, keep straight ahead again to meet it at a pronounced corner of a field with two buildings at its foot. Turn right on to a clear track that leads straight up on to the summit of Table Mountain.

4 Turn off the plateau at its narrowest northern point and cross the saddle on an obvious track. This climbs steeply up on to Pen Cerrig-calch. As the path levels, ignore a track to the left and keep straight ahead until you reach the trig point.

5 Continue ahead to drop slightly down a small crag to meet the escarpment edge. Continue along the ridge, which narrows slightly, then climb again to the narrow summit of Pen Allt-mawr.

6 A path leads down the steep northern spur. Take this and cross flat, open, and often wet ground towards a small hump ahead. As you start to climb, you'll come to a parting of the paths.

7 Fork right here and continue to a small cairn on the top of a narrow ridge that leads southeast. Follow the ridge easily down until you eventually cross some quarried ground and come to a large cairn. Keep straight ahead to walk down to a stile marked 'Footpath Only No Bikes' at the top of a plantation. Cross this and keep straight ahead again to follow the rutted track alongside two sides of the plantation. Where the third side drops away to the left carry straight on over a field eventually meeting a wall to your right that takes you down to a track between walls where you pass through a gate.

8 Go downhill to a junction of paths. Keep straight ahead, through a gate, and head along the top of the field to a marker post pointing left, downhill. Bear left at the bottom to a stile by a gate leading back to the car park.

WHERE TO EAT AND DRINK The Bear Hotel in Crickhowell is the best of the eating and drinking establishments in town. There are other options too.

WHAT TO SEE The tiny town of Crickhowell makes a splendid base for exploration. There are remains of an impressive Norman fortification in the town itself. This was built in the 11th century and became famous after it was attacked by Owain Glyndwr in his uprising of the 1400s. The town's most beautiful feature is the 16th-century bridge over the River Usk.

WHILE YOU'RE THERE Craig-y-Cilau Nature Reserve lies just south of Crickhowell. It features a long limestone crag at 400ft (122m) and there's also a raised bog, woodland and a complex cave system.

Crickhowell and the Grwyne Fechan Valley

DISTANCE 11.5 miles (18.5km)   **MINIMUM TIME** 5hrs 30min

ASCENT/GRADIENT 1,700ft (518m) ▲▲▲   **LEVEL OF DIFFICULTY** ✚✚✚

SEE MAP AND INFORMATION PANEL FOR WALK 38

This is an excellent extension to Walk 38, adding little to the overall ascent but a few scenically stunning miles to the total distance. It delves deeply into the remote head of the Grwyne Fechan Valley, which feels every bit the very heart of the main Black Mountains massif.

Leave Walk 38 at Point **7** by forking left instead of right, to climb easily towards the lower of two humps on the escarpment edge. Pass the boundary stones, now prone but still identifiable by the lettering on them, and drop down to continue north on a clear path that follows the slender ridge. After about 1 mile (1.6km) you'll begin the gentle climb up on to Mynydd Llysiau, Point **A**. The views across the head of the valley are wonderful from here, with Waun Fach lording it over the whole scene and Pen y Gadair Fawr staring back at you from the opposite hillside. To your left is the Rhiangoll Valley, penetrated by the A479, and beyond that the distinctive shoulder of Mynydd Troed and the lengthy upland plateau of Mynydd Llangorse.

Drop down steeply from the narrow summit into a large saddle, marked with a junction of paths and a prominent cairn. Fork right, on to a stony track that drops easily down to a sharp right-hand bend. The more

intrepid may want to carry straight on here to pick up the infant Grwyne Fechan, which can be followed downstream to Tal-y-Maes Bridge. It's very remote and pretty but the going is quite rough and considerably more demanding than the main route described.

Unless you've chosen the harder option, round the bend and follow the broad track down the side of the valley. After a mile (1.6km), meet a dry-stone wall, followed by open moorland again. Eventually you'll drop to the Tal-y-Maes Bridge, Point **B**, a sheltered and scenic spot that makes an ideal place for a rest. Cross the bridge and climb up the opposite hillside on a good track that then bears right to run easily along the top of a succession of fields. The track then drops steeply through a wood and meets the road head at Hermitage. Cross the bridge and head down the road, ignoring the turning on the left, and after another mile (1.6km), you'll arrive back at the start of the walk.

Twmbarlwm and Cwm Carn

DISTANCE 3 miles (4.8km)   MINIMUM TIME 1hr 30min

ASCENT/GRADIENT 1,017ft (310m) ▲▲▲   LEVEL OF DIFFICULTY ✦✦✦

PATHS Clear footpaths and forest tracks

LANDSCAPE Steep-sided, forested valleys, far-reaching views from open hillside near top

SUGGESTED MAP OS Explorer 152 Newport & Pontypool

START/FINISH Grid reference: ST228936

DOG FRIENDLINESS Great dog-walking area, care needed near livestock on Twmbarlwm

PARKING Forest Drive Visitor Centre

PUBLIC TOILETS At visitor centre

It would be difficult to imagine a more transformed landscape than that of the Valleys. Where once slag and spoil heaps towered over bleak villages and greyness appeared to tint everything, there is now every conceivable shade of green, created by mixed forestry clinging determinedly to the steep South Wales hillsides.

The landscapes once scarred by human toil have been returned to the people for leisure. Cwm Carn is only one of many parks in the area that have received this treatment. Its crowning glory is the mighty mound of Twmbarlwm, rising to 1375ft (419m) and enjoying incredible views over the Bristol Channel.

Near Twmbarlwm's characteristic summit – locally known as 'The Tump' or, rather unkindly, 'The Pimple' – are the remains of a hill fort believed to have been constructed by a Celtic tribe called the Silures in the Iron Age or late Bronze Age. Various legends surround the mountain. One maintains that it is the site of buried treasure that is guarded by bees, while another claims that a giant or great warrior slumbers beneath its soil.

The Cistercian Way is an informal 650-mile circular long-distance footpath, the aim of which is to link all the 17 ancient and modern Cistercian abbeys in Wales. First walked in 1998 by Cistercian enthusiasts, the route uses old roads, trackways and pilgrimage paths as much it can, and where this is not possible, opts for the tow paths of canals and disused Victorian tramways. As it careers along the ridge of Mynydd Maen on its circuitous route from Llantarnam to Risca, the Cistercian way passes very close to Twmbarlwm.

Another footpath crosses our route, this one waymarked (with a symbol of a raven). The Raven Walk is an 12-mile circuit taking in the heights around Risca, Cwmcarn, Crosskeys and Ynysddu. Along the route there are four sculptures of ravens, each one concealing a letter from the ancient Ogham alphabet. The four letters, when put together, spell a Welsh word. If you contact the organisers of the walk with this word, you'll be sent a smart enamel Raven Walk badge. And who said walking wasn't a rewarding pastime?

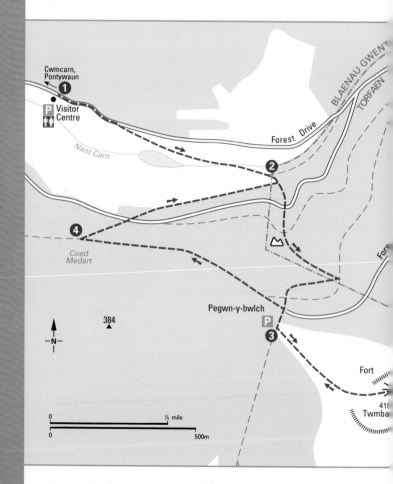

1 From the car park, head up to the visitor centre, and follow the decking around to the right to keep the building on your left-hand side. Go through a gate on to a tarmac footpath and follow this up to Cwm Carn, which was actually built using spoil and debris from the colliery. Walk along either side of the small lake and then, at the far end, continue up a footpath with the stream on

your left-hand side. Pass a little pond on a boardwalk and then, at a timber barrier, cross the stream on a tarmac bridge. Bear around to the right and follow the road up the valley, with a steep grassy bank, once a spoil heap, on your left. Above this, you should be able to make out an old winding wheel, which marks the spot of the colliery's second downshaft.

2 Continue over the stream again, then, with a barrier ahead, bear right through a gate to walk uphill on a narrow path. This ends at a gate, which you don't cross; instead, take the second track on the left. This leads on to the tarmac Forest Drive where you turn right and immediately left, to continue uphill on a broad track. As this bends left, bear right to climb up to the forest drive again. Turn right to follow it down slightly and around a sharp righthand bend. Fork left here, through a gate, on to a narrow trail that leads uphill. Follow this to the Forest Drive again, go through a gate, and turn right to a four-way junction. Take the second of the two left turns and climb to a gate on the left, next to an information board, which leads on to the open hillside of Twmbarlwm.

3 Go though the gate and follow the track steeply up to a bank and a deep ditch that formed the defensive ramparts of a sizeable Iron Age settlement. Continue to the trig point, from where there are fabulous views in all directions, then carry on in the same direction to the strange-looking castle mound at the eastern end of the ridge. The purpose of the mound isn't known, but it's considered to be of Norman construction, from around 1070. Retrace your steps back down to the gate and then the four-way junction where you keep almost straight ahead, down some wooden steps, on to a waymarked bridleway. This drops sharply down through the forest to emerge on a forest track at a hairpin bend.

4 Turn right to the Forest Drive and keep left to come off the road and on to another waymarked bridleway (Raven Walk). Follow this down and then to the right, near the valley floor, to walk above a fence and across the mountain bike trail. This leads to the stile at the five-way junction you passed earlier. Turn left on to the narrow path and walk down to the gate and the information plaque. Cross the stream and turn left to follow your outward journey back to the lake and the visitor centre.

WHERE TO EAT AND DRINK There's an excellent cafe at the visitor centre, which serves up all the usual hot snacks such as soup, jacket potatoes and anything with chips, as well as sandwiches and great cakes. For something stronger, try the Castle Inn in the nearby village of Pontywaun.

WHAT TO SEE The Industrial Revolution had a huge affect on the valleys of South Wales. Limestone, iron ore and coal were found in abundance and in close proximity to each other. Villages and towns sprang up almost overnight. By the early 20th century, over 250,000 men were employed in South Wales, working more than 600 mines. The Cwm Carn Colliery, originally a downshaft for the nearby Prince of Wales Colliery in Abercarn, become an independent mine by 1912 and was expanded in 1914; an engine wheel, close to the walk, marks the spot. Most of the output was shipped to Newport by canal and from there exported to Europe. The colliery finally closed in 1968.

WHILE YOU'RE THERE Caerleon is one of the most significant Roman sites in Europe and worth a visit to see the remains of the centurions' barracks including a well-preserved amphitheatre, of the kind that would have been used to watch the gladiators perform, and a complex system of baths that are remarkably well preserved considering their age. Caerleon is also believed by some to have been King Arthur's court.

Castell Coch and the New South Wales

DISTANCE 5.5 miles (8.8km)	MINIMUM TIME 2hrs 30min

ASCENT/GRADIENT 920ft (280m) ▲▲▲   LEVEL OF DIFFICULTY ✦✦✦

PATHS Forest tracks, disused railway line and clear paths, short section of tarmac

LANDSCAPE Mixed woodland and open hillside with views over residential and industrial developments

SUGGESTED MAP OS Explorer 151 Cardiff & Bridgend

START/FINISH Grid reference: ST131826

DOG FRIENDLINESS Care needed near livestock; not allowed in castle

PARKING Castell Coch

PUBLIC TOILETS In castle and nearby Countryside Visitor Centre

A wooded hillside visible from the M4 motorway is hardly the place that you'd expect to find a fairy-tale castle, but at the bottom of the Taff Vale, just a few miles north of Cardiff, is one that will easily rival those of Bavaria. Castell Coch, with its red sandstone walls and conical towers, is worth a visit in its own right, but perched on a cliff top amid stunning deciduous woodland, it's also a great place to start a walk. Conveniently, two waymarked trails run close to the castle and these, together with a labyrinth of forest tracks, provide an invigorating circular route that shows some of the many different faces of the regenerated Valleys.

CASTELL COCH

Every bit as captivating up close as it is from a distance, the castle was built in the late 1870s on the site of a 13th-century fortress. It had no military purpose whatsoever but was, in fact, a country retreat for the 3rd Marquess of Bute, who at the time was thought to be the richest man in the world and based his empire in Cardiff.

Its design, by the architect William Burgess, is pure, unadulterated fantasy, with a working drawbridge and portcullis, three circular towers and a dream boudoir that features a lavishly decorated domed ceiling. The grandest of all the castle's rooms has to be the drawing room, three storeys high with a ribbed and vaulted ceiling, further decorated with birds and butterflies. The two-storey chimney piece boasts statues of the Three Fates, which show the thread of life being spun, measured and finally cut. Characters from Aesop's fables are also depicted. The route away from the woods follows a section of the Taff Trail, a 55-mile (89km) waymarked route that leads from Cardiff Bay to Brecon via the

Taff Valley, Llandaff, Pontypridd and Merthyr Tydfil. Most of the trail, including the lower section of this walk, is along disused railway lines, along with forest tracks and canal paths. From the Taff Trail, this walk follows an airy section of the 21-mile (34km) Ridgeway Walk (Ffordd-y-Bryniau). It climbs steeply on to the narrow ridge of Craig yr Allt, a spectacular viewpoint which on the one hand feels as wild as the mountains further north, but at the same time gives a raven's-eye view of the industrial side of the valleys.

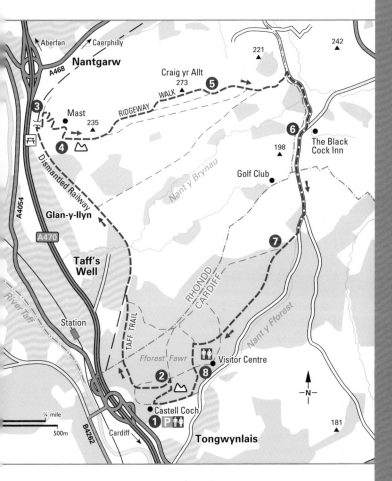

① From the car park, walk up to the castle entrance and turn to the right to walk to a metal information board. Take the path next to this and climb steeply on a good path past a waymark post and through a gap in a fence to a junction of tracks.

② Turn sharp left, signposted 'The Taff Trail', and follow this broad forest track around the hillside and then down, where it meets the disused railway line close to some houses. Pass through the barrier on the right and follow the clear track for over a mile (1.6km) until you pass a picnic area and come to another barrier.

3 Go through the barrier then, as you come to a disused bridge, turn right over a stile, signposted 'Glamorgan Ridgeway Walk'. Take this and follow it for about 76yds (70m) and then around to the right. Ignore one turn left and then turn sharp left to zig-zag back across the hillside, where you turn right again. Follow the main path as it zig-zags up the hillside, aiming at the mast and then, as you reach the field edge, bear right once more. This leads up to a post on a narrow ridge where you turn left.

4 Climb steeply up the ridge and continue, with high ground to your left, until you reach a clear path that leads left by a post, up to the ridge top. Follow this and bear right at the top to walk easily along, with great views. Keep ahead to drop slightly and then bear left on to a broad track that rises up and carries on along the ridge over Craig yr Allt.

5 Follow it down through the bracken ignoring the turn to right. Bear right onto the track down to a kissing gate that leads on to a tarmac drive. Turn left and continue past some houses on the right-hand side to a junction by The Black Cock Inn. Turn right and climb up to another junction, where you bear right.

6 Carry on past the golf club, then fork right on to a narrow lane that drops and bears around to the left. Turn right here to walk past the Forestry Commission sign and then turn left after 54yds (50m), on to a clear footpath marked by a 'no horse-riding' sign.

7 Follow this path, ignoring tracks on both the right and left (two of which are flanked by blue posts), until the posts become blue on your path and you come to a T-junction by a sign forbidding horse-riding. Cross the small brook and turn left to continue steeply downhill, past a turning on the left to the Countryside Visitor Centre.

8 The track eventually swings around to the right and descends to meet the drive. Turn right to climb up the drive and back to the castle.

WHERE TO EAT AND DRINK For tea, coffee and snacks, there's a decent tea room within Castell Coch. For good pub food, stop on your way round at The Black Cock Inn or alternatively, head easily back there once you've finished the walk. To do this, head left out of the car park and bear around to the left at the top of the hill.

WHAT TO SEE Fforest Fawr is a great place in which to spot woodland birds and small mammals, such as the plentiful grey squirrel. Despite being a common and widespread species, the grey squirrel did not occur in Britain before the 19th century. The species originates from North America, and has replaced our native red squirrel across most of Wales since its introduction. Grey squirrels can weigh up to twice as much as red squirrels. They are very active during the day, searching for food on the ground as well as in trees. Contrary to common belief, grey squirrels do not hibernate, and can in fact be seen searching for food at all times of the year.

WHILE YOU'RE THERE Pay your respects by the graves of the 144 people killed by the collapse of a giant spoil heap in Aberfan in October 1966. The horrific landslide engulfed the Pantglas Primary School, burying 116 children.

Sweet Walking on Sugar Loaf

DISTANCE 4.5 miles (7.2km)	MINIMUM TIME 2hrs 30min

ASCENT/GRADIENT 1,150ft (351m) ▲▲▲   LEVEL OF DIFFICULTY ✦✦✦

PATHS Grassy tracks

LANDSCAPE Bracken-covered hillsides, secluded valley and rugged mountain top

SUGGESTED MAP AA Walker's Map 17 Brecon & The Black Mountains

START/FINISH Grid reference: SO268167

DOG FRIENDLINESS Care needed near sheep

PARKING Top of small lane running north from A40, to west of Abergavenny

PUBLIC TOILETS None on route

The Sugar Loaf, or Mynydd Pen-y-fal to give it its Welsh name, is without a doubt one of the most popular mountains in the National Park. The distinctive, cone-shaped outline of the rock-strewn summit is visible from miles around and the convenient placing of a car park on the southern flanks of the mountain makes it easy for those who just want to 'climb a mountain'. To follow the well-trodden trade route is to miss the best of the hill, which, despite its popularity, remains a formidable and dignified peak. This walk takes a more subtle approach, leaving the masses on Mynydd Llanwenarth and dipping into a lonely combe, before making an enjoyable push, up the less-walked west ridge. The steep walls of the valley give a much better sense of scale to the gentle giant you're about to climb. The descent follows the more ordinary route back to the car park.

THE NATIONAL TRUST

The Sugar Loaf, and some of the land that surrounds it, belongs to the National Trust, who own around 4 per cent of the land within the National Park. The Trust was founded in 1895 with the objective of protecting places of beauty and value from the onslaught of industrial development – particularly pertinent in South Wales. It is not, as is sometimes believed, a government-run agency, but a registered charity that relies on membership and donations to carry out its work. The Trust currently acts as a guardian for over 300 historic houses and gardens, 49 industrial monuments, 612,808 acres (248,187ha) of countryside, including the Brecon Beacons' highest peaks of Pen y Fan and Corn Du, and over 600 miles (965km) of coast. It has the statutory power to declare land inalienable, meaning that it can't be sold or purchased against the National Trust's wishes without special parliamentary procedures. Wherever possible, the Trust offers open access to its common land enabling walkers to explore this beautiful landscape at will.

SO MANY SHEEP

Wales has one of the highest densities of sheep in the world. In the Brecon Beacons National Park they outnumber people by 30 to 1. Most of the farms in the National Park are sheep farms. The sheep you'll see while walking across the upland commons are mainly the hardy Welsh mountain sheep, the smallest of the commercially bred sheep with a small head, small ears and a white or tanned face with dark eyes. They thrive in the harsh mountain environment – the ewes spend as many as 36 weeks every year on the high ground – and can eke a living out of the very poor grazing available. Typically, the ewes celebrate the New Year by being returned to the hill – around 80 per cent of them will be carrying lambs. They're scanned for twins in February and those carrying two lambs will be retained on the low ground until they've given birth.

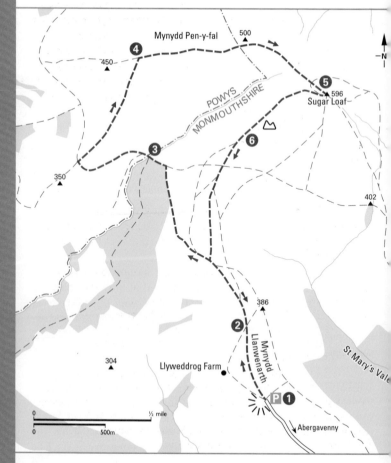

① Standing in the car park and looking up the slope you'll see three obvious tracks leading away. The lowest, down to the left, is a tarmac drive; above this, but still heading out left, is a broad grassy track. Take this and follow it for 500yds (457m) to the corner of a dry-stone wall.

② This marks a crossroads where you keep straight ahead, to follow the wall on your left. Continue along this line for another 0.5 miles (800m), ignoring any right forks, and keeping the wall down to your left. Eventually, you'll start to drop down into a valley, where you leave the wall and head diagonally towards a wood. At the end of the wood, keep left to descend a grassy path to the stream.

③ Climb out of the valley, keeping to the main, steepest, right-hand path. This leads up and around a shoulder and meets another dry-stone wall. Follow this, still climbing a little, until it levels by a corner and gate in the wall. Turn right here, cross some lumpy ground and follow the grassy path up.

④ As the track levels, you'll be joined by another track from the left. Continue ahead and climb on to the rocks at the western end of the summit ridge. Follow the ridge to the white-painted trig point.

⑤ Looking back towards the car park, you'll see that the hillside is criss-crossed with tracks. Most will lead you back eventually, but the easiest route follows a path that traverses right, from directly below the trig point. This veers left and drops steeply down a blunt spur.

⑥ Follow this down until it levels and pass two right forks and a path crossing at right angles. As the track veers left, take the right fork to follow an almost sunken track along a broke wall, which leads to a junction by a wall. This is the track that you followed on the outward leg. Bear left and retrace your steps back to the car park.

WHERE TO EAT AND DRINK The best pub in the area is the Dragon's Head at Llangenny, a few miles from the start. Otherwise, Abergavenny has plenty of options including the excellent Trading Post cafe and the Hen and Chickens public house.

WHAT TO SEE You'll notice from the signage that Sugar Loaf, and much of the land that surrounds it, is owned by the National Trust. The Trust owns over 9,000 acres (3,645ha) in the Brecon Beacons National Park, including the highest summit at Pen y Fan and the dramatic outlier of Ysgyryd Fawr. This is a large area of land but barely a fifth of the Trust's holding in Snowdonia, where it protects over 37,000 acres (14,985ha) of North Wales's most dramatic mountain scenery.

WHILE YOU'RE THERE Between Abergavenny and Monmouth lies a trio of Norman fortifications, White Castle, Skenfrith Castle and Grosmont Castle. They are all managed by CADW and all open to the public during the summer months. White Castle, so named because it was once painted white, is the most impressive and easiest to reach, Skenfrith is in a pretty riverside location and Grosmont sits right on the border with England.

Llanthony and its Hills

DISTANCE 9.5 miles (15.3km)   **MINIMUM TIME** 5hrs 30min

ASCENT/GRADIENT 2,460ft (750m) ▲▲▲   **LEVEL OF DIFFICULTY** ✚✚✚

PATHS Easy-to-follow paths, steep slopes, open moorland, muddy lowland trails

LANDSCAPE Classic U-shaped valleys topped with broad heather-strewn moorland

SUGGESTED MAP AA Walker's Map 17 Brecon & The Black Mountains

START/FINISH Grid reference: SO255314

DOG FRIENDLINESS Some difficult stiles, care needed near livestock. No dogs in grounds of priory

PARKING Narrow pull-in at southern edge of Capel-y-ffin, close to bridge

PUBLIC TOILETS Next to Llanthony Priory

The sheer size of the Vale of Ewyas means that it's best explored in two different walks. The northern reaches are crossed in Walks 48 and 49, while this one tracks south from Capel-y-ffin to loop around the tiny settlement of Llanthony. This circuit passes the ruins of Llanthony Priory and there's a great pub at the halfway stage. The down side is that the head of the valley is some way to the north so, in order to follow both ridges, you'll have to drop into the foot of the valley and then climb out again.

The early stages of both walks follow the same line as far as the crest of the Ffawyddog ridge. From here, this circuit will take you south, over the distinctive serrated skyline of Chwarel y Fan, the site of some disused quarries and, at 2,227ft (679m), the highest point of the day. The ridge then drops steadily down to Bal-Mawr, where you'll follow the banks of the Bwchel brook, through Cwm Bwchel, to the hamlet of Llanthony. From the priory, it's up again, easily at first as you cross the fields adjacent to the ruins, but then steeply to gain a blunt spur that leads on to the slim ridge of Hatterrall. Offa's Dyke Path follows the crest of the ridge, as does the border. Another steep drop brings you back to the pastures above Capel-y-ffin, where you'll pass two tiny, whitewashed chapels before you reach the road.

ANCIENT BOUNDARY

In an attempt to keep the Welsh to the west, King Offa, the 8th-century ruler of Mercia (Central England), marked out his borders with a deep ditch and an earth wall to strengthen natural boundaries such as rivers or ridges. It ran from Prestatyn, on the North Wales coast, to Chepstow, at the mouth of the River Wye. In places it was over 20ft (6m) high and 60ft (18m) wide. Although the official border has changed a little, it still follows a similar line to the original earthworks. Offa's Dyke

National Trail opened in 1971. It follows the north-south line of the dyke for 177 miles (285km) and showcases the incredible diversity of the Welsh countryside.

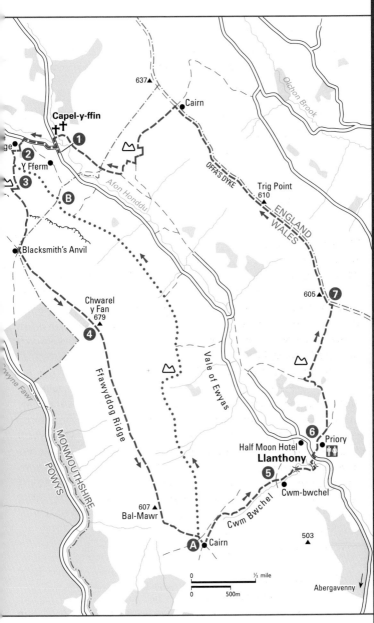

1 Walk towards the bridge, but before you cross it, bear left up a narrow lane, signposted to The Grange Pony Trekking Centre. Follow this along the side of the stream and past a footpath on the left, marked by a stone archway. Continue to a drive on the left, again leading to the trekking centre, and follow this up to a cluster of barns.

2 Keep right here and continue uphill to a large house on the right, with a gate blocking your progress ahead. Bear around to the left and climb on a loose rocky track that leads up to another gate. Pass through this and follow a rough, eroded track as it zig-zags up on to easier ground. Cross the source of a small stream, and continue to the foot of a steep zig-zag track that climbs steeply up the escarpment.

3 Follow this, bearing both right and left and then, as the gradient eases, continue ahead on a broad and often boggy track. Take this past a few small cairns to a large one, the Blacksmith's Anvil, that sits on top of the ridge. Turn left here and continue to follow the track south over Chwarel y Fan.

4 Walk straight on, along the line of the ridge, to reach the summit of Bal-Mawr. Carrying on the same track, go down to the left and pass a good track on your left-hand side. Keep ahead to a cairn and then descend to the left. Drop to a fork where you keep right to follow the brook to a crossroads of paths. Maintain your direction (signposted 'Cwm Bwchel').

5 Cross a stile, down past a house, and over another stile. Ignore another stile on the right and continue down to another at the bottom of the field. Cross this and bear right to cross another and a footbridge. Keep

walking straight ahead to another stile and then continue to a gate. Go immediately through a small metal gate and follow the stream down through another gate to another footbridge. Cross this and take the lane to the road. Turn left here, then turn right to visit the priory.

6 Go through a gate on the left, in front of the priory (signposted to Hatterrall Hill), and follow the main track to a stream, where you turn left to a gate. Continue through a succession of fields, over two stiles and a small copse. Follow the path up on to the ridge and continue to a T-junction; Offa's Dyke is where you turn left.

7 Walk along Offa's Dyke, pass the trig point and continue for another mile (1.6km) to a cairn and a marker stone at a crossroads of paths. Turn left and follow the path down around a sharp left-right zig-zag to a fence. Turn right here, then turn left over a stile. Walk down, over another stile to a hedge at the bottom of the next field, cross another stile and carry on down, before bearing right, crossing a stream and turning left to pass over a stile and onwards onto a tarmac lane. Turn right through a gate and follow this through a yard, where it becomes a rough track. Keep ahead to a sharp left-hand bend and keep straight ahead, up steps and over a stile. Continue straight ahead through more fields to join another lane and follow this down, past two chapels to the road. Turn left to return to your car.

WHERE TO EAT AND DRINK The Half Moon Hotel in Llanthony is worth a visit. This traditional pub is very popular with walkers.

WHAT TO SEE Llanthony Priory dates back to the 6th century AD, when St David himself founded a chapel. The building seen today was constructed in the 12th century as a religious sanctuary for the Norman knight William de Lacey.

Views from Chwarel y Fan

DISTANCE 7 miles (11.3km)   MINIMUM TIME 4hrs

ASCENT/GRADIENT 1,250ft (381m) ▲▲▲   LEVEL OF DIFFICULTY ✦✦✦

SEE MAP AND INFORMATION PANEL FOR WALK 43

While there's no doubting the beauty of the vale between Llanthony and Capel-y-ffin, Walk 43 may be a bit much for some people as it twice makes the strenuous climb from the valley floor on to the surrounding hillsides. A much easier circuit can be made by following the walk along the Ffawyddog ridge, above Llanthony, and then using an excellent contouring track that returns you gently to the finish. Although it's only 2.5 miles (4km) shorter than Walk 43, it almost halves the amount of ascent, making this walk a much more casual proposition.

Follow Walk 43 to the cairn, beyond Bal-Mawr (Point **Ⓐ**) and turn left to drop down, around the hillside, on a broad track that leads easily through the heather. You'll pass above two distinct cwms, which drop down into the valley to your right, but keep straight ahead for just over a mile (1.6km), where the path crosses a brook and bears around to the right, past some tumbledown walls. The track, which is easy to follow, goes steeply down the side of the small valley and then swings around to the left, where it levels out considerably to cross the steep hillside.

Shortly after this, you'll pass through a metal gate that leads into a wooded enclosure and then another that leads back out on to the hillside. Carry straight on, eventually dropping to join the wall that defines the bottom of the open hillside and the top of the pastures. Your navigation worries are over now and the views are great. You can actually see more from down here than you could from the ridge-top path above. Follow the path above the wall for over 1.5 miles (2.4km) until you drop to cross a small brook and climb up beneath a dry-stone wall on your left. This wall circumnavigates a strange marshy dip in the ground that makes a wonderful sheepfold and also offers perfect shelter, should you wish to take a break. Ignore the path leading to a stile on the right and the track off to the left as path turns right, hugging the wall.

From here (Point **Ⓑ**), continue with the bottom wall still on your right until you eventually come back to the open area you passed on the way up, with the zig-zag path that leads up on to the ridge above you to the left. Cross the stream ahead and simply retrace your earlier footprints back down past the pony trekking centre and on to the road.

Overleaf: Llanthony Priory (Walk 43)

Abergavenny's Historic Transport Links

DISTANCE 3.5 miles (5.7km)	MINIMUM TIME 1hr 30min

ASCENT/GRADIENT 160ft (49m) ▲▲▲   LEVEL OF DIFFICULTY ✦✦✦

PATHS Clear, well-surfaced tracks and paths

LANDSCAPE Mixed woodland and tranquil canal banks

SUGGESTED MAP AA Walker's Map 17 Brecon & The Black Mountains

START/FINISH Grid reference: SO262134

DOG FRIENDLINESS Family walkways so scoop the poop

PARKING Small car park at start, south of Govilon

PUBLIC TOILETS None on route

This delightful little walk, by far the least strenuous in the book, follows the lines drawn by two of the area's main 18th- and 19th-century transport arteries. The outward leg follows the now defunct Merthyr, Tredegar and Abergavenny Railway, often known as the 'Heads of the Valleys Railway'.

In places the line follows the path of the much earlier Bailey's Tramroad, which ran from Crawshay Bailey's Ironworks at Nantyglo to Govilon Wharf on the banks of the canal. The initial construction, which stretched between Abergavenny and Brynmawr, was started by the Merthyr, Tredegar and Abergavenny Railway Company. This was then acquired by the London and North Western Railway, who were keen to gain a foothold in South Wales, where they saw the immense profit potential of the 'black gold'. They extended it to Merthyr Tydfil. The line opened in 1862 and closed in 1958. It now forms part of the Govilon to Abergavenny Community Route.

The return leg winds along the tow path of the Monmouthshire and Brecon Canal, originally known as the Brecknock and Abergavenny Canal. Built between 1797 and 1812, it represents a remarkable feat of engineering, with over 23 miles (37km) of its total 33 miles (53km) being level – amazing when you think of the mountainous terrain that it traverses. Linking Brecon with Newport and hence the Bristol Channel, the canal was used to transport stone and processed lime from local quarries.

On 16 October 2007, the canal burst its banks near Gilwern, sending a mini-Niagara down into the Usk valley. People had to be evacuated from nearby houses and it was declared that a 16-mile section of the canal would have to be drained in order for the banks to be thoroughly inspected. The repairs took 17 months and many millions of pounds but the canal was finally re-opened on 29 March 2009. It is now home to several narrowboat hire companies, including one which operates Britain's only electric fleet. These can be re-charged at various points along the canal and are extremely popular with holidaymakers.

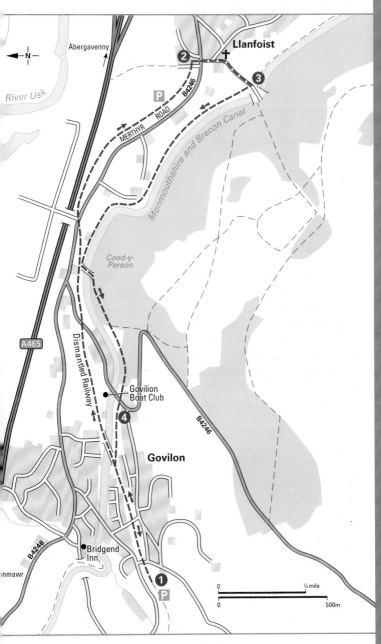

❶ A clear tree-covered track runs parallel to the car park. Go through the barrier on to it and turn left. This is now the line of the railway. Follow it beneath a bridge to a residential road and go straight across, around a barrier. Continue behind a row of houses. The path then vaults the canal on a bridge that you should note as it marks the spot where you leave the waterside on the return leg. Continue parallel to the canal for a while, then duck back into woodland, keeping straight ahead at a junction, waymarked right to the canal. The path passes beneath deciduous trees made up mainly of oak, birch and ash. You're likely to see many small birds, especially those of the garden variety, including most members of the tit family, robins and wrens.

❷ About 1.25 miles (2km) after crossing the canal, you'll come to a gate and a car park on the outskirts of the small village of Llanfoist, which grew up on the transport links of the area. Its lime kilns were fed by limestone quarried on the flanks of Blorenge and brought down to the canal by another tramway. Turn right, cross the main road and walk up the lane opposite. This passes the church on the left and climbs steeply up towards the canal. As the lane swings sharply left bear right to climb steps up onto the tow path.

❸ Turn right and continue along the bank, which is particularly beautiful in autumn when the magnificent beech woods show off a full spectrum of autumn colours. After about a mile (1.6km), you'll cross a bridge to continue on the south bank, with some canalside houses taking prime waterfront locations opposite. Shortly after this you come to the Govilon Boat Yard, where an interpretation board maps out many interesting facets of the canal's history. Govilon, like its neighbour Llanfoist, came about because of its position between the natural resources of the mountains and the developing transport network. It was ideally positioned to receive stone from Clydach, which was then transferred to the canal by tram.

❹ Pass the impressive boat club and another attractive waterside building and then, at the bridge, fork left to follow a well-surfaced path away from the canal and around to the right. This path leads back on to the disused railway where you bear left to follow it back into the residential area and on to the car park.

WHERE TO EAT AND DRINK The Bridgend Inn in Govilon is a lively, comfortable place, which serves good beer and excellent food that varies from the exotic to its own famous beef and dripping sandwiches.

WHAT TO SEE As you walk along the banks of the canal, look out for a glimpse of one of Britain's most colourful birds, the kingfisher. In flight, the diminutive little hunter appears less like a bird and more like an ethereal flash of luminescent blue that resembles something from a fairy-tale. It nests in tunnels in the riverbank and generally lays six or seven white eggs.

WHILE YOU'RE THERE See some more of the canal by either hiring a boat from one of the many operators or alternatively take a half-day cruise from Brecon – Dragonfly Cruises operate from the Canal Basin area near the theatre. It really is a relaxing way to see the countryside.

Bird's-eye View of Abergavenny

DISTANCE 3 miles (4.8km)	MINIMUM TIME 1hr 30min

ASCENT/GRADIENT 530ft (162m) ▲▲▲   LEVEL OF DIFFICULTY ✦✦✦

PATHS Clear tracks over open mountainside, quiet lane

LANDSCAPE Rugged mountain scenery, huge views over Usk Valley

SUGGESTED MAP AA Walker's Map 17 Brecon & The Black Mountains

START/FINISH Grid reference: SO270109

DOG FRIENDLINESS Care needed near livestock and on road

PARKING Small car park at Carn-y-gorfydd

PUBLIC TOILETS None on route

There's no easier peak to climb in the Brecon Beacons National Park, but there are also few that occupy such a commanding position. The Blorenge – the English-sounding name probably derives from 'blue ridge' – towers menacingly above the cramped streets of Abergavenny, with the main sweep of the Black Mountains leading away to the north. The mountain actually dominates a small finger of the National Park that points southwards from Abergavenny to Pontypool. It's unique in being the only real peak south of the A465 Heads of the Valleys road. It also marks a watershed between the protected mountain scenery that makes up the bulk of the National Park and the ravaged industrial landscape that forms the southern boundary. Typically, its northern flanks boast a Bronze Age burial cairn and the ground above the escarpment is littered with grass-covered mounds, a remnant of past quarrying. The stone was then transported away on the canals and railways.

Commonly seen as the eastern gateway to the park, Abergavenny is a thriving market town that owes its success to weaving, tanning and farming. It feels a thousand miles away from the industrial valleys that nudge against its limits from the south. The name, which in Welsh means the confluence of the River Venny, refers to its position at the junction of the River Fenni and the River Usk, but oddly, in Welsh, it's known simply as Y Fenni - the name of the river.

NORMAN CASTLE

Abergavenny sprang up around a Norman castle built to rid the area of the Celts. Dirty tactics were used to achieve this, such as inviting the Welsh leaders to dinner and then murdering them while they were unarmed. The castle is now a museum with some interesting displays of the town's history. Another of Abergavenny's claims to fame is the fact that during World War II, Hitler's deputy, Rudolf Hess, was imprisoned here after his plane crashed in Scotland.

IRON TOWN

Only 5 miles (8km) south of Abergavenny, but culturally and spiritually a completely different world, Blaenavon tells the full, uncut story of industrial expansion in South Wales. With iron ore, limestone, coal and water all found in local abundance, smelting began here as early as the 1500s, but the town, and the huge iron works that came to dominate it, didn't really get going until the Industrial Revolution of the late 18th century. The colliery, now known as the Big Pit Mining Museum, was founded a full century later than the iron works and only closed as recently as 1980. It has been immaculately preserved and well organised to give visitors a meaningful insight into the industry itself, the conditions that the people endured and the culture that grew up around them. As well as the engine houses, workshops and the

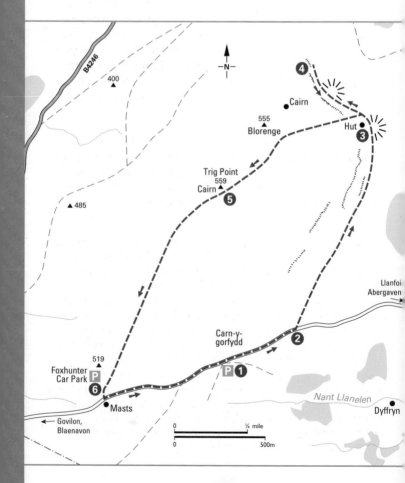

miners' baths, a tour, usually accompanied by a genuine ex-miner as a guide, includes donning a miner's helmet to descend one of the shafts to the actual coal-faces. Blaenavon is considered such an exceptional example of industrial South Wales that it was declared a UNESCO World Heritage Site in 2000.

1 From Carn-y-gorfydd Roadside Rest, walk downhill for 500yds (457m) and bear left, through a green barrier, on to a grassy track.

2 This leads easily uphill, through a tangle of bracken, eventually allowing great views over the Usk Valley towards the outlying peak of Ysgyryd Fawr.

3 As the path levels you'll pass a small locked hut. Continue along the escarpment edge, on one of a series of terraces that contour above the steep escarpment, and enjoy the views over Abergavenny and the Black Mountains. The rough ground was formed by the quarrying of stone.

4 Return to the hut and bear right, on to a faint, grassy track that crosses flat ground and a small boggy patch before climbing slightly and becoming stony. Away to the right, you should

be able to make out the pronounced hump of a Bronze Age burial cairn. The path now leads easily to the trig point and the huge cairn that mark the summit.

5 Continue in the same direction, drop down past an impressive limestone outcrop and towards the huge masts on the skyline. You should also be able to see the extensive spoil heaps on the flanks of Gilwern Hill, directly ahead. A few hundred metres from the trig point look out for the tentative beginnings of a grey gravel path (lined, towards the end, with 'Heather and Heritage' waymarkers) that will take you all the way to the car park.

6 At the masts, you'll cross the Foxhunter Car Park to meet the road where you turn left and continue easily downhill, for 600yds (549m), back to the start.

WHERE TO EAT AND DRINK The Bridgend Inn in Govilon was built in 1786 and is the main pub in the village. Meanwhile the Lamb and Fox at Pwlldu is a low-ceilinged affair with an open fire and the only building left of an abandoned village. There's also plenty of choice in Abergavenny town.

WHAT TO SEE This is one of the best places in South Wales to see and hear red grouse, which were once managed on these moors. The size of a pheasant, without the long tail, the male is a rusty reddish brown colour and the female more buff and mottled. You'll usually be alerted to their presence by a stabbing, alarmed clucking, followed by a short frantic escape flight.

WHILE YOU'RE THERE Blaenavon is well worth visiting. As well as the iron works and Big Pit Mining Museum, there's also the incredibly scenic train ride along a short section of the Pontypool and Blaenavon Railway, the highest standard-gauge track in Wales today. It stops off at the Whistle Inn, a nostalgic miner's pub that would have once taken its fair share of the modest wages paid to the men at the face.

Superb Views from Ysgyryd Fawr

DISTANCE 3.75 miles (6km)   MINIMUM TIME 2hrs

ASCENT/GRADIENT 1,150ft (351m) ▲▲▲   LEVEL OF DIFFICULTY ✦✦✦

PATHS Tracks through woodland and bracken, steep climb and easy traverse of airy ridge

LANDSCAPE Mixed woodland, bracken-covered slopes, views over Black Mountains

SUGGESTED MAP AA Walker's Map 17 Brecon & The Black Mountains

START/FINISH Grid reference: SO328164

DOG FRIENDLINESS Care needed near livestock

PARKING Small car park at start

PUBLIC TOILETS None on route

NOTES Do not attempt this walk after a period of prolonged rainfall

Ysgyryd Fawr, or Skirrid Mountain as it's also known, is the easternmost peak in the Brecon Beacons National Park. Isolated from the Black Mountains by the Fenni Valley, it's perfectly situated to offer superb views over the rest of the range.

This is a short walk, but it's not to be underestimated; after an easy but enjoyable ramble around the western flanks, the route to the top makes a direct assault on a steep spur that offers little quarter in the fight against gravity. It's definitely worth the effort though, as the summit gives stunning views and the slender ridge that marks the line of descent is one of the finest skyline walkways in the area. However, coming down off the summit can be very muddy and quite dangerously slippery after a protracted rainfall, so do not attempt to do this walk during rainy periods.

YSGYRYD FAWR

The mountain has long been referred to as the Holy Mountain. The deep cleft in the ridge is said to have been created by a freak bolt of lightning at the time of the crucifixion and the soil in the valley that divides the hillsides is thought to have special powers. It has even been said to have originated in the Holy Land or, at the very least, Ireland, imported by St Patrick himself. History records local people collecting the soil to sprinkle on anything from coffins to fields of crops. The evangelical importance of the mountain was marked with a small medieval place of worship, dedicated to St Michael, and squeezed on to the narrow summit. Years of mountain-top weather have taken their toll and only the outline plus two small stones that form a doorway remain. There's also evidence of a small hill-fort on the same spot. The name Ysgyryd probably derives from *Ysgur*, Welsh for 'divide', and *Fawr* meaning 'great' or 'big'. You'll find its little sister Ysgyryd Fach, ('small') a couple of miles further south, on the outskirts of Abergavenny.

THE BRECON BEACONS NATIONAL PARK

The Brecon Beacons National Park was founded in 1957 as one of ten across England and Wales. It's the second-largest of the three in Wales, the largest being Snowdonia and the other, the Pembrokeshire Coast. Stretching from Llandeilo in the west to Abergavenny in the east, and between Llandovery and Hay-on-Wye on the northern boundary and the heads of the industrial valleys that define the southern perimeters, the Brecon Beacons National Park covers a total area of 519 square miles (1,344sq km).

The majority of the land is privately owned, but around 14 per cent belongs to the National Park Authority, 8 per cent to the Forestry Commission and around 4 per cent is National Trust land.

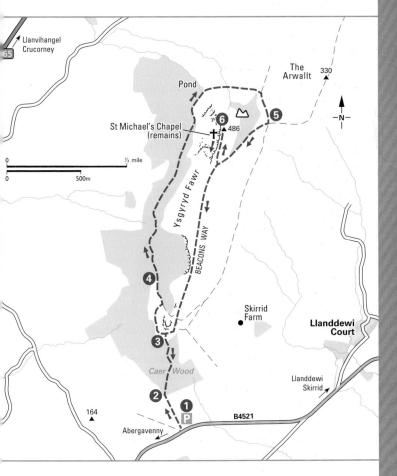

1 Walk through the barrier at the western end of the car park and follow the hedged track around to the right. Climb up to a gate and stile beneath a large oak tree. Cross these and follow the green and white waymarker that directs you off to the right.

2 Ascend a few wooden steps and keep straight ahead at a staggered crossroads, again following the green and white marker posts. You'll cross a grassy forest track and then climb a series of steps to cross another forest track. Continue to a gate.

3 Turn left here and follow the moss-covered wall around. The wall drops to the left, but continue along the path.

4 This now undulates as it contours around the hillside, eventually leading into a narrow rock-strewn valley. Stay on the main path to pass a small pond on the left and gradually veer around to the right. Stay on the path and you'll emerge on to open ground with a fence to your left. Continue until your way ahead is blocked by a gate.

5 Fork right in front of the gate and follow the open ground steeply uphill. Stay on the main path, following National Trust markers (watch out for the second one which is very small and off to the right of the path), and eventually you'll reach the top of the ridge. Turn right and follow the ridge for a few paces to the summit.

6 To descend, retrace your steps back to the point where you joined the ridge and then keep straight ahead to the end. Drop down the narrow southern spur and bear around to the right to join a stone path. Follow this down to a wall and bear right to return to the gate at Point **3**. Retrace your steps back down through the wood to return to the car park.

WHERE TO EAT AND DRINK Considering how remote it is, there's a couple of good options for this walk. East, in Llanddewi Skirrid, there's the Walnut Tree Inn, a smart restaurant with rooms, and north, in Llanvihangel Crucorney, there's the Skirrid Inn, purported to be the oldest pub in Wales and also haunted by the ghost of a rebel who was hanged there.

WHAT TO SEE There are a few places on this walk where the path has been constructed using lumps of local stone, laid in such a fashion that vegetation will eventually re-establish itself around them. Footpath erosion is a huge problem across the whole of the Brecon Beacons. Boots destroy vegetation and the thin layer of topsoil is then easily washed away by rainwater, forming deep trenches. It's important to follow these reinforced paths wherever they are found and also to avoid widening any existing tracks by cutting corners or by bypassing puddles and bogs. If you see white bags scattered across the hillsides anywhere, these are full of stone for the paths and have been dropped there by the Ministry of Defence, who use the Beacons for training exercises.

WHILE YOU'RE THERE This is the nearest walk in the book to Raglan Castle, a few miles east of Abergavenny. Raglan was the last medieval fortification to be built in Britain and it remains in surprisingly good condition, with an impressive moat and hexagonal Great Tower.

The Vale of Ewyas Horseshoe

DISTANCE 9 miles (14.5km)	MINIMUM TIME 4hrs

ASCENT/GRADIENT 1,560ft (475m) ▲▲▲   LEVEL OF DIFFICULTY ✦✦✦

PATHS Easy-to-follow tracks, steep slopes, open moorland

LANDSCAPE Classic U-shaped valleys, broad heather-strewn moorland

SUGGESTED MAP AA Walker's Map 17 Brecon & The Black Mountains

START/FINISH Grid reference: SO255314

DOG FRIENDLINESS Great for dogs but care required near livestock

PARKING Narrow pull-in at southern edge of village, close to bridge

PUBLIC TOILETS None on route

The steep clamber out of Capel-y-ffin will make you short of breath, but don't be put off. Once you've made the giant cairn that marks the top, the rest is child's play and the views, as you cruise comfortably along the giant whaleback that makes up the Ffawyddog ridge, are just superb. At Pen Rhos Dirion, you nudge over 2,296ft (the 700m contour on OS maps) and reap the fruits of your labour with a sweeping panorama over the Wye Valley. East is Twmpa, often referred to as 'Lord Hereford's Knob', and beyond that, the Gospel Pass and Hay Bluff – the eastern end of the impressive Black Mountains escarpment. The head of the Ewyas Valley is split in two by a rugged slither of upland known as Darren Llwyd. This offers an airy return route with views to the east that match the earlier vista to the west. The spur drops away sharply at its southern tip and your eyes will be drawn straight ahead, where the Ewyas displays the classic U-shape of its Ice Age roots.

BOOK CITY

This walk is near to the small town of Hay-on-Wye, which can be seen clearly from the northern escarpment. Known as the 'second-hand book capital of Wales', if not the world, the town marks both the northernmost point of the National Park and also the Anglo-Welsh border, with Herefordshire to the east and Powys to the west. Like many of the towns in the area, Hay-on-Wye grew up around its impressive Norman castle, which was built on the site of an earlier motte-and-bailey construction. This was all but destroyed by Owain Glyndwr, the statesman-cum-warrior and self-declared Prince of Wales, during his crusades of 1400. These days the town's deepest history is almost forgotten and the colourful municipality has reinvented itself as a bustling, cosmopolitan settlement with an upbeat feel that is totally different from the neighbouring farming communities.

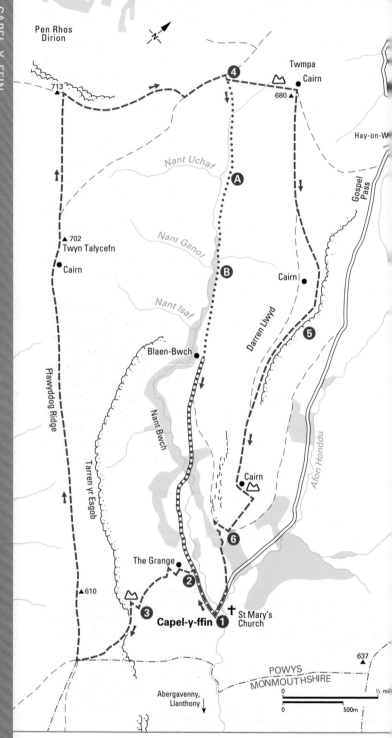

Pen Rhos
Dirion

713

Twmpa
Cairn

680

Hay-on-W

Nant Uchaf

A

Gospel Pass

702
Twyn Talycefn

Cairn

Nant Ganol

B

Cairn

Nant Isaf

Darren Llwyd

5

Ffrawddog Ridge

Blaen-Bwch

Nant Bwch

Cairn

Afon Honddu

Tarren yr Esgob

Cairn

610

6

The Grange

2

3

Capel-y-ffin

1

St Mary's
Church

POWYS
MONMOUTHSHIRE

637

Abergavenny,
Llanthony

0   ½ mil

0   500m

1 Walk towards the bridge, but before you cross it, bear left up a narrow lane, signposted to The Grange Pony Trekking Centre. Follow this along the side of the stream and past a footpath on the left, marked by a stone archway. Continue to a drive on the left, again leading to the trekking centre, and follow this up to a cluster of barns.

2 Keep right here and continue uphill to a large house on the right, with a gate blocking your progress ahead. Bear around to the left and climb on a loose rocky track that leads up to another gate. Pass through this and follow a rough, eroded track as it zig-zags up on to easier ground. Cross the source of a small stream, and continue to the foot of a steep zig-zag track that climbs steeply up the escarpment.

3 Follow this, bearing both right and left and then, as the gradient eases, continue ahead on a broad and often boggy track. Take this past a few small cairns to a large one that sits on top of the rounded ridge. Turn right and follow the track easily over Twyn Talycefn to the trig point on Pen Rhos Dirion. (The summit can be avoided by a clear path that traverses left before the final climb.) Turn right and drop steeply down through the heather into a broad saddle.

4 Keep straight ahead over the flat section and then climb steeply up on to Twmpa. Turn right here and then, for maximum effect, bear left on to a narrower track that follows the line of the eastfacing escarpment. Stay with this track until the ridge narrows and drops steeply away.

5 Descend directly to a large square cairn, then keep ahead to continue down a steep spur and as it becomes too steep to continue, zig-zag left then right, to cut a steep line through the bracken to a junction with a broad contouring bridleway. Keep straight ahead to cross this and drop down to pick up a narrow stony track that runs along the side of a wood.

6 After the wood, ignore a grassy path that crosses obliquely. Shortly afterwards turn left almost back on yourself to follow this down to a stile and keep straight ahead to pass between two houses. When you reach the drive, keep straight ahead to cross a stile and continue in the same direction to cross another stile in the bottom corner. Turn right on to a lane and follow it to return to your car.

WHERE TO EAT AND DRINK You have a choice depending upon which way you're heading. Over the Gospel Pass you'll find the cosy Three Horseshoes in Felindre, which is well known for its good food and drink. Or, while heading south, there's the Half Moon Hotel in Llanthony village which is definitely a walkers' favourite.

WHAT TO SEE The tiny chapel at the end of the walk is St Mary's Church, one of the smallest in the country, with an interior that measures only 26ft (7.9m) by 13ft (3.9m). It was built in 1762, and the porch was added 55 years later. There are galleries along the west and south walls and an octagonal pulpit. The belfry, which is decidedly lopsided, houses two bells.

Vale of Ewyas: Along the Course of Nant Bwch

DISTANCE 7 miles (11.3km)   MINIMUM TIME 3hrs 30min

ASCENT/GRADIENT 1,360ft (415m) ▲▲▲   LEVEL OF DIFFICULTY ✛✛✛

SEE MAP AND INFORMATION PANEL FOR WALK 48

From Point ④, continue easily across the saddle until, just before you start to climb again, a clear grassy path crosses the track. Bear right here and follow the path down into a narrow niche at the head of a pronounced valley. The track then follows the east bank of the small stream down.

The interest for most people on on this walk is definitely to your right where, after 0.5 miles (800m), a narrow, secluded valley hurdles a few rocky steps to empty into the Nant Bwch. This is Nant Uchaf (Higher Brook), the first of three such tributaries, hewn out of the otherwise barren moorland, that drain into this stretch of the stream, Point ④. The other two are rather predictably named Nant Ganol (Centre Brook) and Nant Isaf (Lower Brook).

Just before you reach Nant Ganol, keep a sharp eye open for a path that leads to a pronounced meander in the river. Here, you'll find a delightfully positioned grassy glade, which presides over a small waterfall. This is as fine a spot for a picnic as you are likely to find in this area. Immediately downstream of the falls, the Nant Ganol makes its appearance to your right, again pouring over a small waterfall, this one framed by birch trees, Point ⑧.

Rejoin the main path and continue down to a gate, which marks the end of the riverside walking. Follow the fenced track down to another gate and a remote farmhouse, where it picks up the road. All that remains is an easy, downhill stroll, back into Capel-y-ffin and your car.

WHILE YOU'RE THERE Hay-on-Wye really took off in 1961 when Richard Booth opened a second-hand book shop in the town. Somehow, his business exploded and soon other booksellers set up shop here. Today there are over 30 of them with Booth's being the largest, containing over half a million books. He didn't stop here either. Disillusioned with the inefficiency and bureaucracy of large government organisations that, in his opinion, were doing little or nothing to prevent rural jobs from being lost, in 1977 he declared Hay-on-Wye independent from the rest of the UK, and appointed himself King. The highlight of the town's calendar is the Hay Festival of Literature, which takes place every May.

Break for the Border

DISTANCE 8 miles (12.9km)   MINIMUM TIME 3hrs 30min

ASCENT/GRADIENT 820ft (250m) ▲▲▲   LEVEL OF DIFFICULTY ✦✦✦

PATHS Excellent, waymarked forest tracks and paths

LANDSCAPE Steep-sided wooded valleys

SUGGESTED MAP AA Walker's Map 14 Wye Valley & The Forest of Dean

START Grid reference: SO533001

FINISH Grid reference: SO534938

DOG FRIENDLINESS Care on main roads. Dogs not allowed in abbey or castle

PARKING Tintern Abbey

PUBLIC TOILETS Car park at start of walk and near Chepstow Castle

The Wye Valley Walk is a 136-mile (218km) waymarked recreational trail following the River Wye as it meanders between Plynlimon in mid-Wales to Chepstow on the banks of the Severn. By making use of public transport, this walk takes in one of the most beautiful and historic sections, between Tintern Abbey and Chepstow. The number 69 bus runs roughly every two hours between Chepstow and Tintern.

Tintern Abbey was only the second Cistercian monastery founded in Britain and the first ever in Wales. Building works began in 1131 and continued on and off right up to its dissolution four centuries later. Its most captivating feature is its Gothic church, begun in 1269 and completed 32 years later. The lord of Chepstow Castle, the wonderfully monikered Roger Bigod, rebuilt the church completely in the late 13th century and even in its ruined state it retains a majestic quality. The monastery flourished, despite the depredations of the Black Plague in 1348-49 and the unsettling effects of the Welsh uprising in 1400-15, up until 3 September 1536 when it was surrendered to King Henry VIII.

Built just a year or two after the Norman Conquest, Chepstow Castle was not made of timber, as would generally have been the case around 1067, but of stone. One of William's most trusted henchmen, William Fitz Osbern, had a keep constructed on a ridge above the River Wye. It is now Britain's oldest surviving stone keep.

Around 1200, a bailey was added by William Marshall in what was then the new-fangled round style. This was followed over the next century by the addition of curtain walls, barbicans and gatehouses, vastly extending the castle until it dominated the entire ridge. Roger Bigod III then added a 'D' tower so strong that the castle was used defensively until 1690 when, after it fell twice to the Roundheads during the War of Three Nations, further adaptations had to be put in place to ward against cannon fire. Today the castle is at last at peace and well worth a visit at the end of the walk.

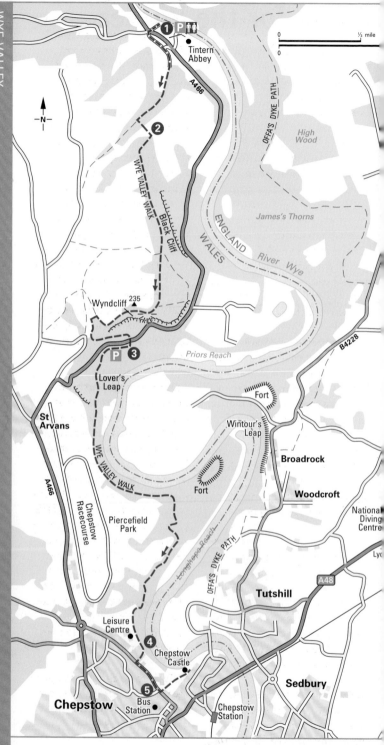

1 The best way to join the Wye Valley Walk (WVW) from the abbey is to head out of the car park, the way you came in, and keep straight ahead to hug the river bank on a drive that runs between houses, and then bear left past a converted church. This leads up to the main A466, where you'll see two small lanes heading uphill opposite you. Take the left lane (as you look at them) and follow this uphill until it ends and you bear right up a stony track. Keep heading up through a canopy of beech trees until, after 0.5 miles (800m), you see a waymarker that directs you across a small stream on the left. Cross this and follow the narrow path up to a gate that leads on to an open hillside. Cross the field to another gate that takes you back into the wood.

2 Turn immediately right and the path now steepens and carries you up on to a narrow wooded ridge above Black Cliff. Bear left when it levels to climb steeply again, then continue for another 0.75 miles (1.2km) to a crossroads of paths. Keep straight ahead to continue above Wyndcliff to a fingerpost that directs you to the airy viewpoint of Eagle's Nest. The river curls in a series of giant loops beneath your feet and you should be able to see the limestone cliffs of Wintour's Leap on the far bank. These are popular rock climbing crags and also mark the route of the Offa's Dyke footpath, which runs along their tops. Head back up to the main path and continue to a car parking area, where you turn sharp left to go downhill, via a series of zig-zags, to the A466. Cross the road to another car parking area.

3 Keep right, parallel to the road, and locate the path, which at this stage is gravel and runs down into the wood next to a Wye Valley Walk information board. The gravel soon gives way to leaf litter and beechnuts and the noise of the road is quickly left behind as you delve deeper into the wood. After a short and particularly rough section of path you'll find yourself cruising easily along a narrow terrace above the steep-sided valley. In common with most deciduous woods, there's plenty to capture the imagination at any time of the year, but it's certainly at its best when bathed in the rustic colours of autumn, or in spring when the forest floor is carpeted with flowers and the trees ring with the sound of birdsong. You'll pass behind Piercefield Park and duck into a short, claustrophobic tunnel cut into the rock. Ignore the path off to the right shortly afterwards and continue to a junction with another track, where you turn right then drop to the left of this.

4 A viewpoint by a bench marks the end of the woodland section of the walk and from here, a set of steps leads up to a gap in a wall. Go through and follow the path as it leads behind a leisure centre and out to a car park. Turn left on to the main road and follow it downhill to a narrow park opposite a turning called Kingsmark Avenue. Turn left on to the waymarked footpath and pass the castle on your left. The Great Tower Keep was built by the Normans in 1067, just one year after the Battle of Hastings. Take time to have a look around and then turn right by the tourist information centre to emerge on Bridge Street.

5 Turn right to climb up through the High Street to reach the bus station and take the number 69 bus back to the start of the walk.